T0003330

A
CHRISTIAN
JUSTICE
FOR THE COMMON GOOD

Other Abingdon Press Books by Tex Sample
Earthy Mysticism: Spirituality for Unspiritual People
Blue Collar Resistance and the Politics of Jesus
Hard Living People & Mainstream Christians
Powerful Persuasion: Multimedia Worship in Christian Witness
White Soul: Country Music, the Church and Working Americans

A
CHRISTIAN
JUSTICE
FOR THE COMMON GOOD

TEX SAMPLE

Abingdon Press
Nashville

A CHRISTIAN JUSTICE FOR THE COMMON GOOD

Copyright © 2016 by Abingdon Press

All rights reserved.

This book is printed on acid-free paper.

Library of Congress Cataloging-in-Publication Data has been requested.

ISBN: 978-1-5018-1426-6

Scripture quotations unless noted otherwise are from the Common English Bible. Copyright © 2011 by the Common English Bible. All rights reserved. Used by permission. www.Common EnglishBible.com.

Scripture quotations marked NRSV are from New Revised Standard Version of the Bible, copyright 1989, Division of Christian Education of the National Council of the Churches of Christ in the United States of America. Used by permission. All rights reserved.

16 17 18 19 20 21 22 23 24 25—10 9 8 7 6 5 4 3 2 1
MANUFACTURED IN THE UNITED STATES OF AMERICA

I am deeply indebted to the efforts of the following organizations in Kansas City, Missouri, that work faithfully in the pursuit of a justice of the common good. This book is dedicated to them.

Communities Creating Opportunity

The Human Dignity and Economic Justice Coalition

The Metro Organization for Racial and Economic Equity

The Urban Summit

Workers for Justice

CONTENTS

ACKNOWLEDGMENTS

"Much obliged" was a phrase I grew up with. You don't hear it much anymore. It was something said in appreciation for a favor done, a courtesy given, or an offer extended. It is a good word for my indebtedness in this book. I am the beneficiary of many friends, both personal and public. These acknowledgements are a brief way to express my gratitude for their gifts and the ways they have blessed my life.

First, I thank those who read part or all of the manuscript, good friends all: Alice Blegen, John Blegen, Sam Mann, Joe Rubio, Robert Day Sartin, and Paul Turner.

I especially appreciate the work that editor David Teel did on the manuscript. He encouraged me to do additional writing in places where it was clearly needed. The book is better because of his good eye and thoughtful responses. His support is equally valued.

Work on the topic of a Christian justice for the common good began in two lectures I did for the Desert Southwest Conference of the United Methodist Church in 2012. I thank Bishop Minerva Carcano for her invitation to make these presentations and to the Conference Board of Church and Society, who sponsored the event to which I spoke.

In 2013 I gave the Fall Convocation Lecture for the Garrett Evangelical Theological Seminary. I am grateful to its president at that time, Phillip Amerson, who asked me to make the presentation that is reworked and extended here as chapter 1 and chapter 6.

I am indebted to the Vanderbilt Divinity School and its Dean Emilie M. Townes, who invited me to give the Cole Lectures in 2014. Chapters 3 and 4 of this book are a reworked version of the material I presented there.

Over the last three years I have spoken in dozens of local churches and at denominational events on aspects of the thoughts herein. I am ever grateful for the hospitality extended to me by these groups across the country.

For the last sixteen years I have worked steadily and for many hours in interfaith and community organizing efforts that inform what is here. I want especially to mention the following: the Arizona Interfaith Movement and the Valley Interfaith Project in Phoenix, Arizona, and in Kansas City, Missouri: Communities Creating Opportunity, the Human Dignity and Economic Justice Coalition, the Metro Organization for Racial and Economic Equity, the Urban Summit, and Workers for Justice. I am grateful for all the ways they have shaped and mentored me. I dedicate the book to the Kansas City organizations with whom I have more recently worked.

For the last year and a half I have served as an interim pastor for Trinity United Methodist Church, then the Keystone and Revolution United Methodist Churches, and now the Blue Ridge Boulevard United Methodist Church. These pastorates have given me the opportunity to carry out learnings "down on the ground" of parish life. My only regret is that I have been pulled away from our home church, The Grand Avenue United Methodist Church.

Finally, I made the "mistake" of marrying a woman I really like, meaning by that that I never get to spend as much time with her as I would wish. Peggy Sample is that rare combination of beauty and warm affection, of artistic sensibilities and extraordinary empathy, and of an intuitive intelligence and a practical bent. That I got to marry and spend my life with her blows my mind.

PREFACE

Justice has been a major concern of my adult life, and I have been heavily involved in broad-based organizing for the past sixteen years. Beginning with the civil rights movement in the sixties, much of my work focused around a justice of rights. Yet I am aware that as crucial as human rights are, they are not enough. Increasingly I find myself working from the Christian grounding of my commitments where my primary passion and conviction lie. The deepest wellsprings of my life reside in the confident persuasion that God has acted centrally in Jesus Christ to disclose God's Self and to change the course of history.

At the same time, I find myself engaged with Jews, Muslims, agnostics, atheists, and those of other traditions. These relationships and their signal importance to justice work in the community and beyond find me working for a justice of the common good, which is where I spend most of my time. It is this passion for a Christian justice and my investment in a justice of the common good that animates this book, hence the title, *A Christian Justice for the Common Good*.

In these pages I attempt to address these two basic concerns. In the first chapter, I sketch out a Christian justice based in the righteousness of God as found in God's act in Jesus Christ. I draw here explicitly from the writings of the Apostle Paul. In these terms Christian justice is a radical alternative to the justices of other traditions. Indeed, I find no other faith tradition constituted in these ways.

In the second chapter I face the challenge that a Christian justice requires a rigorous formation of our sensibilities and dispositions, and I attempt to embody these in stories of people so cultivated and forged. Explicitly I look at the way we see, hear, smell, taste, and touch, and at the centrality of dispositions of nonviolence to our formation as just people.

Basic to this formation are the practices of language, and in chapter 3 I examine the important role of talking the talk and do so in a closer look at the skills of language in a Christian justice. Talk is often discredited in Christian witness and justice, and I challenge this depreciation and maintain that language is the very stuff of life and that justice requires the use of language as craft, suggesting some of the practices of this trade.

This, of course, is not to disparage walking the walk. So in chapter 4 I address skills related to the physical and embodied practices of a Christian justice, again focusing on the skills of this work with attention to matters like know-how, apprenticeship, showing up and turnout, sizing up situations, and scut work. I conclude this chapter with a discussion of an alternative view of the self as a subject to be formed, an understanding of freedom as talkability and walkability, and a comment on grace.

Chapter 5 speaks to two key issues in the work of justice, self-interest and power. Working with the account of interests by Albert O. Hirschman, who reports the shifts in the meaning of the concept across the last five hundred years in the West, I make the case for interest as story- and tradition dependent. I then connect this understanding of interest to Augustine's position on the loves in *The City of God*.

Next in chapter 5 is consideration of Bernard Loomer's relational understanding of power, very much in the tradition of broad-based organizing. I extend this view, however, by drawing on the philosopher Michel Foucault and the anthropologist Talal Asad to move to a more concrete analysis of power through close examination of the practices in which it is exercised. The implications of this analysis are next examined not only in terms of influencing others but also with regard to how we form and change ourselves.

In chapter 6 I face into the fact that we live in a world with others, people of other faith traditions and those of no faith traditions. In relating to these others I draw explicitly from stories of Jesus and explore Paul's instruction that we are to seek the good of all. From these I describe the common good as a discovery that is built from the ground up working with flesh-and-blood people, in this case, in a broad-based organizing approach. To give more concreteness to this approach I summarize briefly the cycle of organizing and its use in the community and also in the local congregation.

In chapter 7 I then discuss connections between a Christian justice and a justice of the common good to conclude the book.

This is not an academic book. Excellent studies of a Christian justice already exist, and I cannot improve on them.[1] Although I hope academics

---

1. See, for example, Daniel M. Bell Jr., *Liberation Theology after the End of History* (New York: Routledge, 2001) and Luke Bretherton, *Christianity and Contemporary Politics* (Chichester, West Sussex, UK: Wiley-Blackwell, 2010).

will read what is here, this work is written for those who have serious interest in a Christian justice and the common good but come out of a more church- and community orientation to these topics. This book aims at an audience of community activists, clergy, informed laity, and college and seminary students seeking to engage these important matters.

I use a lot of stories, not to substitute narrative for argument but rather to be as concrete as I can be. I want to embody the claims made here so that these pages can be focused down on the ground in the thickness of people's lives. John Milbank says, "Narrating is a more basic category than explanation or understanding."[2] I agree. In language there is no substitute for the materiality, the corporeality, the tangibility, the nuts and bolts, and the plot line of story. I have tried to be faithful to this claim here.

---

2. John Milbank, *Theology and Social Theory*, 267.

Chapter 1

A CHRISTIAN JUSTICE

I remember the sixties as the baby boomer generation came of age into their late teens and twenties. We began to hear expressions that I had not heard before. Things like, "Do your own thing," "If it feels good, do it." "Do it now!" "Do whatever floats your boat." "Do whatever turns you on." "You can do whatever you want so long as you do not get in anyone else's way of doing what they want," and so on. Such phrases seemed to have great currency then, at least with the boomers.

Those sayings, however, greatly diminished in the following decades, and I have a "theory" about why that language, though it did not disappear, nevertheless lost considerable currency in the seventies and eighties. In my "theory" I argue that once baby boomers had fourteen-year-old children, they ceased, or at least greatly curtailed, their use of such claims. It became clear, it seems, that something terribly risky or inappropriate or just down-right foolish came with such language when applied to their own children.

Now, let's cut the boomers some slack. They were born following World War II into a very different world, a society, as Daniel Yankelovich claimed, of such affluence as the world had never known up until that time in history. The United States had not sustained the damage to its industrial infrastructure that the nations of Western and Eastern Europe and Japan and other Asian countries had. The United States stood at the apex of the industrial world, with an economy that was producing "the affluent society," as was boasted at the time.[1]

Boomers were the beneficiaries of that affluence, and they were the subjects of an advertising campaign on a scale never known before, especially with the onslaught of television. If a consumer society commodifies

---

1. Yankelovich, *New Rules*, 21–24. In this book, however, Yankelovich, writing in the early eighties, recognized that the economy was going through a serious economic reversal since the mid-seventies. The term *affluent society* comes from John Kenneth Galbraith, *The Affluent Society.*

everything, that process was under way, and boomers were powerfully influenced by it.

Boomers also were born into a time when human rights were taking on powerful expression, not only in the civil rights movement but also in those protesting the Vietnam War and those giving expression to the counter-culture movement. Boomers were, of course, active participants in all of these momentous events.

There is a relationship between the affluence of that time and the movements for human rights. I want to connect the dots between the human rights movement and the boomer sayings with which I began this section. But I do not want to be misunderstood. I fully support human rights and believe them utterly necessary if we are to give people even relative protections from the encroachments of the nation state and the economic order of capitalism, indeed, from the captivities of any of the principalities and powers that dominate the infrastructure and horizon of our lives. To forsake human rights is to play the fool in today's world, indeed, in any world I can foresee.

A JUSTICE OF RIGHTS VERSUS A JUSTICE OF THE COMMON GOOD

But there are problems when justice is reduced to one of human rights, because taken alone, human rights cannot sustain the rich realities of a justice of the common good, not to mention the even more fulsome character of a distinctively Christian justice, or the kinds of justice one finds in Judaism or Islam, as other examples.

Let me suggest, then, first, that the grave danger today is the impact of a consumer culture with its commodification of human rights into an individualistic expressivism. That is, if human rights are understood as individuals doing whatever they please so long as it does not interfere with the choices of others, then we have not only no commitment to the common good but not even a conception of it, except by default—that is, whatever happens as a result of our not getting in the way of each other's individualistic wishes. If all we do is protect individuals in doing whatever turns them on, we have nothing but "free autonomous individuals" pursuing *wants* now defined as rights.

Let me be clear, it is neither my wish nor the plan of this book to constrict human freedom. As much as I question an individualistic expressivism,

I do not trust coercion, especially on matters of personal decision. At the same time, we need a far more profound understanding and practice of justice, and, I might add, an understanding of freedom that exceeds the narrow confines of mere choice. Even more, we need a populace formed and committed to the common good and to the policies and procedures for its discovery and fulfillment.

Further, a good deal of the political shenanigans and inequalities of the market are directly related to the absence of a widely shared commitment to the common good. While the concentrations of power in both government and the market are basic to our problems, commitments to the common good have an impact even on power distributions. Commitments to the common good, the eminence of such language, the way that our concepts shape our experience, and the politics of an aroused and concerned citizenry can certainly call into question and bring redistributions of runaway power. We are not damned to the status quo. In later chapters I hope to show some of the directions for this kind of civic action.

Second, when justice is reduced to human rights, there seems to be an unexamined faith in a preestablished harmony of outcomes if people merely pursue their individualistic choices and expressive whims. It presumes that if you do what you want to do and I do what I want to do, things will work out just fine. This harks back to Adam Smith's confidence about invisible hands that operate in a free market and is a shibboleth of those neoclassical economic true believers who maintain that such a dynamic operates to bring about the greatest good of the greatest number. Nobel Prize winner and economist Joseph Stiglitz states that "Adam Smith's invisible hand—the idea that free markets lead to efficiency as if guided by unseen forces—is invisible, at least in part, because it is not there."[2]

What free market advocates of this kind refuse to see are the concentrations of power that occur in the market where deregulations occur on the scale that neoclassical legislation and policy promote. Not only that, these concentrations of power in the economy lead to concentrations of wealth that give big corporations control and influence over politicians and elected officials with the result that we lose a government of the people, by the people, and for the people. A powerful critique of the control of Congress by the wealthy and the necessity of campaign finance reform comes to us from David Cay Johnston. He describes the vast network of subsidies, giveaways, and legal absolutions that serve the wealthy and corporate America,

---

2. Stiglitz, "There Is No Invisible Hand."

a network that distributes income up at the cost of flesh-and-blood, workaday Americans.[3]

But, more than that, a justice of rights requires some vision of the good if it is to escape the development of an individualistic expressionism that loses a sense of community and fails to build broad commitments to the common life. When such occurs, community becomes increasingly fragmented and the result is the building of lifestyle enclaves and identity politics.

Martin Luther King Jr. led one of the great human rights movements of the last century. Yet, it must not be missed that his vision—his conception of the common good—was one of *beloved community*, which inspired his work and called him beyond a justice of rights alone. His own sense that rights were not enough is portrayed in a story told by Harry Belafonte.

On March 27, 1968, just eight days before his assassination, King was at a party at Belafonte's home. In a conversation during the party King got in an argument with Andrew Young, who would eventually be the mayor of Atlanta, about the proposed Poor Peoples Campaign in Washington, DC. Belafonte reports King's passion for the event and his troubled frustration over the fact that he and the younger people in the movement could not agree on tactics, although King asserted that he shared their rage, pain, and frustration. He agreed with the younger activists that the problem was the system.

Young replied to this comment, "Well, I don't know, Martin. It's not the entire system. It's only part of it, and I think we can fix that."

King, angered by this remark, rebuked him, "I don't need to hear from you, Andy. I've heard enough from you. You're a capitalist, and I'm not. And we don't see eye to eye on this and a lot of other stuff."

After what Belafonte describes as "an awkward moment," King went on to argue that "we live in a failed system." He criticized the unequal distribution of economic resources, and the way this system serves the rich at the expense of the poor. He observed that the wealth of the rich "exceeds conscience and almost all others are doomed to be poor at some level." King concluded his argument stating that the system had to be changed and that it would not change itself. "We're going to have to change the system."

After a reflective moment when he spoke of the hard-won gains of the civil rights movement, he paused and said, "But what troubles me now for all the steps we've taken toward integration, I've come to believe that we are integrating into a burning house."

---

3. Johnston, *Free Lunch*. See especially 283–98.

4

Belafonte noted that the group "had not heard Martin quite this way before. I felt as if our moorings were unhinging." He blurted out, "Damn, Martin! If that's what you think, what would you have us do?" "I guess we're just going to have to become firemen," answered King.[4] This deep unrest with a program of human rights alone increasingly characterized King's last years. For example, he realized that getting people the right to enter a cafe where they could not afford to purchase a meal was no final answer. He understood the system required a more encompassing good that went well beyond rights alone. Fundamental systemic wrongs were at work, notably in America's involvement in the Vietnam War, in the unjust distributions of wealth and income, and in the unrelieved poverty that characterized so very many black, white, and brown people. For these reasons, among others, he was planning the Poor People's Campaign in the weeks before his death.

Third, a justice of rights taken alone does not build character. Simply endorsing people's claims to pursue their preferences does not develop in people the sensibilities, the dispositions, the structures of feeling, and the commitment to each other necessary to a common good. A justice of rights without character is little more than a consumerist construction, the commodification of people into the utilities of the market.

We are formed by our practices, both those of language and those of our other activities. So a language of individualism and preferential rights wedded to pursuits that are limited mainly by noninterference with the proclivities of others become the form of life into which people are invested, habituated, and shaped.

In sum, a justice of human rights, as necessary as it is, provides a grossly inadequate form of justice. It leads to an individualistic expressivism that reduces rights to wants, to a freedom of mere choice, and neglects commitment to and service of the common good. A justice of rights, moreover, has an unjustifiable faith in a preestablished harmony of outcomes that cannot be defended or sustained. It results rather in the fragmentation of community into lifestyle enclaves and a politics of identity. Further, it does not build character nor the kinds of human beings required for a community for and of the common good.

To close out this section, let me say that a justice of rights fails to take advantage of the rich faith traditions and their teachings and practices of justice. I include here the traditions of atheism, for example, which is its

---

4. Belafonte, *My Song: A Memoir*, 326–29. I am indebted to Sam Mann for calling my attention to this scene in Belafonte's book.

own kind of faith tradition. In my community activities I grow increasingly concerned that Jews, Christians, Muslims, Buddhists, atheists, agnostics, and others find themselves addressing issues in terms of human rights and often avoid the rich perspectives and practices of justice from their own traditions. This means not only that we miss out on the treasures of millennia of discourse and practice but that the deepest wellsprings of devotion are excluded from the public square as well.

It is out of these concerns about the limitations of a justice of rights and the need for the extraordinary contributions that can be made from different faith traditions that I turn now to a distinctively Christian view of justice with the aim of naming specific understandings and approaches that grow from this form of life. As a Christian I find this to be the most compelling and encompassing approach to justice. It concerns me that often in the church justice is understood in one of two ways. For some, the gospel is understood in such individualistic ways that salvation is seen as saving single souls into heaven and that the purpose of church is subverted by calls to justice because they're seen as "politics."

For others, it seems that justice is largely a consequence, an implication, a secondary concern, or an activity that grows from the more central events of what God has done. On these views, God's work in Christ justifies us by divine grace and our faith becomes active in love. From this we then hear expressions like "justice is love distributed,"[5] or "justice is what love does when you have more than one neighbor,"[6] or "justice is the order that love requires."[7] Such views suggest that justice is a derivative of love and often secondary to what God has done in Christ.

As central as love is in the Christian faith, I shall argue that justice lies at the very heart of God's revelation in Jesus Christ. My focus here will be especially on the writings of the Apostle Paul. I shall argue that in Paul's gospel justice is not a derivative or an implication of the human response of love but rather that justice is central in the revelation of God and that any effort to make it somehow a consequence of our responding to God has missed the centrality of justice in the very initiative of God, in the very disclosure and action of God in the world.

Let me be clear, I have absolutely no interest in diminishing the towering importance of love in the Christian faith. It is clear, God's love and our loving response to that divine grace is central and not to be qualified. My

---

5. Joseph Fletcher, *Situation Ethics*, 99.
6. Paul Ramsey, *Basic Christian Ethics*, 243.
7. Daniel Day Williams, *The Spirit and Forms of Love*, 250.

focus, instead, is to place the issue of justice in the initiative of God, specifically in divine righteousness. As Paul says in Romans, "He also did this to demonstrate that he is righteous in the present time, and to treat the one who has faith in Jesus as righteous" (3:26). That is, a Christian justice finds its character in the disclosure and action of God's righteousness. It is out of this conviction that I turn now to substantiate this claim through a brief summary of Paul's account of righteousness.

GOD'S REVELATION: DISCLOSURE AND COSMIC HISTORICAL CHANGE

There is a terrible tendency in the Christian West to individualize the writings of the Apostle Paul. There is, perhaps, no better place to see this than the way the Greek New Testament word *dikaiosune* is translated into justification in English and then used to understand justification in Paul's gospel as one of saving individuals. We have heard it a thousand times; it goes like this. God has demonstrated saving love on the cross, and God's grace is available to all who will confess their sin, accept forgiveness, receive and trust God's grace, and respond in faithful living. In this framing of Paul's gospel, we often hear that we are to have a personal relationship with Jesus Christ.

There could hardly be a more anemic misreading or misinterpretation of Paul's writing. To be sure, God's grace, the cross, and the call for our response are powerfully central to Paul's gospel, but this individualized misreading fails to appreciate the cosmic and historical sweep of Paul's proclamation.

The very center of Paul's gospel is God's revelation (Greek, "apocalypse" in Jesus Christ. This revelation of God is, indeed, a disclosure of God, of God's grace, of God's great love for the world. Yet, in Paul, it is even more. God's revelation in Christ is a cosmic, historical act of God. Not only has God disclosed Self, but God has changed the world and altered history. The world will never be the same again.

To convey the radical character of this divine action, J. Louis Martyn names God's act an "invasion" of the cosmos.[8] Why an invasion? Because in Paul the basic human problem or condition—indeed, the problem of the cosmos itself—is not that we need to be forgiven for our sins. It is rather that the world and we ourselves are enslaved to powers beyond our control.

---

8. Martyn, *Galatians*, see 343–52, especially 349.

We are not able to break this captivity, to free ourselves. More than this, confinement goes beyond some existential captivity of human life alone. For Paul the entire cosmos is enslaved, with this captivity taking on a supernatural character.

THE POWERS IN PAUL

When Paul uses words like *sin, flesh, elemental spirits,* and *death,* he is describing the range of our captivity. Let us look at his use of these four concepts. Notice that he seldom uses the word *sins;* his word is *sin,* which suggests not individual acts or transgressions alone but some larger, incarcerating power that holds us in its grip. Sin is not only a personal matter, though it is that. It can set up a military-like readiness or fortification in us (Rom 7:11). It masters human beings as an enemy full of guile, by which we are overmatched, too impotent to counter and overcome it (Rom 7:8-11). Sin can even take over something good like the law and by that work "death in me," says Paul (Rom 7:10-13). Sin takes away our very agency so that the good we would do, we do not do. We can even will what is right but we cannot do it. "I don't know what I'm doing, because I don't do what I want to do. Instead, I do the thing that I hate" (Rom 7:15). For Paul there is a war in his "members" between the "law of God" and the "law of sin" from which he cannot rescue himself (Rom 7:21-25 NRSV).

Paul's use of the word *flesh* is not to be equated with our bodies. For Paul the body is part of creation and it is good. The word *flesh* speaks instead to how our bodies are enslaved to powers beyond ourselves. To live life in the flesh is to be dominated by sinful passions (Rom 7:5); it is to "sow to the flesh" and thereby "reap corruption" (Gal 6:8 NRSV), which results in its destiny of death.

The concept of *elemental spirits* in Paul reflects a traditional view of the cosmos in the ancient world. On this traditional view the world is made up of polarities such as earth and air, fire and water. These oppositional pairs give the world its foundation, structure, and order. In Paul's writing, however, we find new kinds of opposites such as Law/Not Law, circumcision/uncircumcision, and Gentile/Jew, slave/free, and male/female polarities (Gal 3:28).[9] Beverly Gaventa understands these polarities as undermined and superseded by the new creation brought by God's action in Christ. People no longer find their identity in terms of religious, ethnic, economic,

---

9. Martyn, *Galatians,* 272–73, 376–78.

social, and gender status. Rather, the rankings of the old creation are obliterated. People are moved to a new and different place, from the spaces of "Torah observance, or slavery or gender into the new world of Christ."[10] Finally, *death* itself is a power. In Romans 5:12–8:2 we find Paul's most sustained account of death. Here Paul tells us that death came into the world by sin through the transgressions of one man, Adam (5:12), but death dominates everyone, and all are condemned because all have sinned. So the power of sin rules in death (5:21) as the wages of sin (6:23), with death as the final and destructive consequence of sin. Death is the great enemy and the final dominant power, yet, just as Adam's trespass led to condemnation for all, the faithful obedience of one man, Christ, leads to the justification of all made righteous by his crucifixion and resurrection (5:18-21). The ultimate and final defeat of death will be accomplished when Christ comes again, and we wait for that time when "the creation itself will be set free from slavery to decay and brought into the glorious freedom of God's children" (8:21).

It needs to be understood that in Paul these powers take on a supernatural character. Words like "rule" (*arche*), "authority" (*exousia*), and "power" (*dynamis*) refer to cosmic or heavenly spheres and forces that stand as enemies in opposition to God (1 Cor 15:24; Rom 8:38; see also Col 1:16; 2:10-15; Eph 1:21; 3:10). At the same time, scholars affirm that Paul's position on the powers also has this-worldly political implications. When Paul proclaims that Christ is Lord, he declares that all the kingdoms of this world belong ultimately to God, that every ruler, authority, and power will finally be destroyed, and that all will finally come under divine rule. This stands as a direct challenge to the power, authority, and rule of the Caesars of Rome.[11]

BETWEEN THE TIMES

Paul is convinced that all of these powers have been decisively defeated in Christ's crucifixion and resurrection. Even so, this defeat of the powers is not complete. Paul acknowledges that we continue to struggle while we await the final victory over the powers in Christ's return. He assures the church in Rome that he believes "the present suffering is nothing compared to the coming glory that is going to be revealed to us." The creation has

10. Gaventa, *Our Mother Saint Paul*, 68.
11. See Hays, *First Corinthians*, 265. Hays is working here with Witherington's book, *Conflict and Community in Corinth*, 295–98.

been subjected to futility, and the whole creation groans in labor pains until now while we wait for adoption and for the redemption of our bodies (Rom 8:18-24).

Here it is important to understand this already/not yet dimension of Paul's writing. He is clear that already the powers have been defeated in God's cosmic and historical act in Christ. In this sense we know how the struggle between God and the powers ends, but in Paul's writing we await the final victory that comes with the *parousia*, "the return of Christ." Understood in these terms, we live between the times, between the time of Christ's coming and that of his coming again. We live between the already and the not yet (1 Cor 1:4-9, 11:26; 15:20-28).

In broad-based organizing, which I shall consider later, there is a distinction between the world as it is and the world as it ought to be. I read this to be one way to express Paul's understanding of living between the times. In organizing there is ever this sense of being between the world as we find it and a more normative vision.

Theologian William Cavanaugh uses Richard Strauss's opera *Ariadne auf Naxos* to express this idea of living between the times.[12] In the opera the richest man in Vienna builds a grand house and wishes to celebrate its completion with a feast for many guests. He decides, first, that the celebration will present the performance of a tragedy, with that followed by a comedy, and then conclude with a fireworks display. To say the least, the composer of the tragedy is not a little put off by his work being followed by a comedy, but this is the richest man in Vienna, and the composer complies.

But things get worse; the wealthy host becomes concerned that the evening will go on for far too long. Further, the story of the opera is one in which Ariadne, the heroine, has lost her lover and has consigned herself to Naxos, a stark, desolate island, where she will await death in her unrelieved grief. Understandably, the wealthy host is concerned not only about the length of the evening as planned but about the depressing effect of the tragic plot of the opera. Therefore, to save time and to change the mood of what is supposed to be a celebration, he decides to have the tragedy and the comedy performed concurrently both to counter the mood of the tragedy, on the one hand, and to provide ample time for the fireworks, on the other.

So, as the performance of the tragedy proceeds, the comedienne Zerbinetta bursts on the scene with her retinue of harlequins, nymphs, and buffoons. In her role Zerbinetta has such clarity about her own identity that she is always herself in every scene, but she also possesses a high competence

---

12. Cavanaugh, *Migrations of the Holy*, 63–65.

in improvisation of a kind that would please any jazz devotee. As a result she and her comedic troupe continually break into the tragedy, interrupt its plot, and enact an alternative story line. Then, into this contest between tragedy and comedy comes Bacchus, a god from heaven, with whom Ariadne falls in love, and who takes her away to heaven where they live and love happily forever.

Comedy, of course, is a play or story or event where things turn out right; in tragedy things turn out badly or wrong. I love Cavanaugh's use of Strauss's opera as an analogy for the church living between the times. We are the comediennes, or—which I like even better—the clowns. We are that odd lot called to infiltrate the narrative of the powers, to wiggle our way into the plot line, and to embody and proclaim a different story. We are those who make do, who muddle through, often without adequate resources. We extemporize, never clear about what comes next, but confident ultimately about how the story ends. We are called to be clowns for Christ, to do stand-up comedy to counter the tragedies of the world.

I do not mean to suggest that we take the tragedies lightly or ignore the immense suffering that goes on. Basic to our call is a response to these profound hardships and to alleviate need and damage wherever we can. At the same time, we are the people convicted that the tragedies of the world do not have the last word.

THE NEW CREATION

This is a good place to address a key duality in Paul's writing, that of old creation and new creation. As we have seen, the old cosmos has been crucified and a new creation has begun in God's disclosure and history-altering action in Jesus Christ. In Galatians 3:28 the old polarities of Jew or Gentile, slave or free, and male and female are no longer. Instead, God has brought forth a new community/assembly, a people called to be an alternative to the "present evil age" (Gal 1:4), a community that finds its identity and its mission not in conformity to the world but rather by being transformed through renewal of the minds of its members and by their bodies becoming living sacrifices to God (Rom 12:1-2).

This charismatic community, delivered from the captivity of the powers, partakes of the faith of Christ and is empowered by the Spirit to be obedient to God as Christ was obedient in going to the cross. Freed and empowered to be instruments and slaves of righteousness, this assembly is equipped with a variety of gifts by the Spirit, and every member of the body is now given "a demonstration of the Spirit . . . for the common good" (1 Cor 12:7). Paul's metaphor or image for this assembly is "the body of Christ," an assembly characterized by its participation in Christ, a body made up of many members but still one body (Rom 12:4-5).

Participation in the body of Christ is a rich and complex dynamic of relationships in Paul. Christ resides in the hearts of believers (Gal 4:6), and forms their life in community (Gal 4:19). Belonging completely to Christ, the ecclesia serve him who now rules the new creation (Gal 5.25). Further, baptism is an act in which believers are incorporated into Christ and take him on like clothing (Gal 3:27). Note, too, in Paul's dispute with the Corinthians where he takes them to task over the Lord's Supper, he asks, "Isn't the cup of blessing that we bless a sharing in the blood of Christ? Isn't the loaf of bread that we break a sharing in the body of Christ? Since there is one loaf of bread, we who are many are one body, because we all share the one loaf of bread" (1 Cor 10:16-17).[13] Finally, though not exhaustively, the members of the ecclesia take on a unity beyond their national identity and worldly status: all "were . . . baptized by one Spirit into one body, whether Jew or Greek, or slave or free, and we all were given one Spirit to drink" (1 Cor 12:13).

These few comments only touch the rich array of uses of participation in Paul's work but should be enough for my purposes here. With this necessarily brief overview of Paul's gospel, we are now able to examine the key role of righteousness in his writing. This will provide the basis for the development of a Christian view of justice.

JUSTIFICATION OR RECTIFICATION

J. Louis Martyn in his commentary on Paul's letter to the Galatians argues that *dikaiosyne*, the word usually translated "justification" in Paul's writings, should be translated rectification. He demonstrates convincingly that God's righteousness, revealed in God's act in Christ, has put or set right Jew and Greek, slave and free, and male and female. On Martyn's reading rectification is the righteousness of God, God's justice, the act of God in Christ by which God has set right both the cosmos and history.[14]

It is crucial here not to turn *dikaiosyne* into an individualistic instance of God forgiving a sinner and, by God's grace and the sinner's trustful acceptance of that grace and forgiveness, becoming saved. This is a gross

---

13. See Martyn, *Galatians*, 573.
14. Ibid., 97–105, 263–80.

misreading of Paul's message. It is necessary to understand Paul's gospel as one of deliverance, where all of humanity, the cosmos, and history have been set free from the captivity of the powers.

Redemption for Paul is one of release from captivity where one enters the ecclesia, that new creation set loose in the world by the power of the Spirit to proclaim that the walls of hostility are defeated. We are empowered to stand on those walls by God's grace, to declare they no longer matter, and to live out and embody a ministry of reconciliation.[15]

It is my contention that a Christian view of justice will draw its character from this understanding of *dikaiosyne* or righteousness. Hence Christian justice will not reside fundamentally in human rights or some other set of human claims but in the character of what God has done in Christ. My job here, therefore, is to name key characteristics or dimensions of the divine righteousness that are to be embodied and performed by the church as the new creation.

This means, again, that justice is not a derivative of human responsive love—and certainly not an individualistically conceived love—wherein we resort to definitions of justice: justice is what happens when we have more than one neighbor[16] or justice is the order love requires[17] or justice is love distributed.[18] This is not to deny the importance of love as having a role in justice but rather that justice resides at the heart of God's revelation in Christ. Before we love God and neighbor in response to God's action and grace, the constitution of justice is housed in the very initiative of God's work of redemption. I turn now to that.

A CHRISTIAN JUSTICE

Dan Bell makes the claim that in a Christian approach "Jesus in his person *is* the justice of God."[19] I think that claim is right on. If we are to take seriously the revelation of what God has done in Christ, then a Christian work of justice will seek a description of justice in terms of God's revelation. Too often we have attempted to derive justice from the instruction that we

---

15. To be sure, Paul does deal with individual transgressions or sins. He does so by providing an approach for the ecclesia, which has a role in dealing with such transgressions. See Gal 6:1-10.
16. Ramsey, *Basic Christian Ethics*.
17. Williams, *The Spirit and Forms of Love*.
18. Fletcher, *Situation Ethics*.
19. Bell, "Jesus, the Jews, and the Politics of God's Justice," 97.

are to love neighbor as self. Part of the problem here is that justice then becomes some utilitarian attempt to love more than one neighbor, or seek some order required by love, or distribute love to a wide range of neighbors. Of course, it is certainly not my point that love has nothing to do with justice. Rather, in the same way that love is portrayed for us in God's revelation in Christ, so it must be with justice. It is not human-responsive love to God that defines justice but rather God's revelation in Christ—God's righteousness—that does so. In my attempt to address justice in these terms, I will continue to draw on Paul's gospel and name three characteristics of God's revelation in his writing.[20]

Redemption/Liberation

Even in so brief an account of Paul's gospel as I lay out above, it is clear that God's work in Christ—God's righteousness—is one of setting humanity and the cosmos free from the enslaving powers that hold the creation in their grip. God's act in Christ is one of deliverance. This act of deliverance has already occurred in Christ, and we await the ultimate fulfillment in Christ's return.

Further, this deliverance is a far more encompassing action by God than the kind of individualistic reductionism committed by those who understand redemption only as saving individuals for eternal life, that is, going to heaven. Paul's thought here is as wide as the cosmos; it encompasses the entire creation. To turn such good news into saving only individuals fails to see the magnificent work God has done in Christ and will do in God's ultimate completion of the creation.

Still, there is more. The church as new creation is that peculiar body called to proclaim this gospel of deliverance from the powers. The powers build a world of walls and make those walls sometimes look natural—as the way things just are. Sometimes those walls appear utterly victorious and invulnerable—obedience to them seems simply to be "realistic." But we are those who can stand on those walls and declare that they finally do not win. We are those made free by God in Christ to cross the walls of the world and to name this the living out of the future. Indeed, it is to live the future in the here and now. It is to insert ourselves in all the wrong places for all the right reasons.

---

20. I am indebted here for these three characteristics to Stanley Hauerwas. See "Jesus, the Justice of God," *War and the American Difference*, 99–116. Hauerwas is, of course, not responsible for the way I use and develop these characteristics.

In 1984 an escaped inmate from a Tennessee prison showed up in the early morning hours at the house of Nathan and Louise DeGraffenreid in Mason, Tennessee. Nathan had stepped outside their house with a cup of coffee in his hand when suddenly he felt the point of a pistol barrel shoved into his back. The intruder directed him to go back inside, as the gunman followed.

Once inside, the stranger was confronted by Louise who gave him a direct order to put the gun down because, she said, "We don't allow no guns in this house." She told him she was going to fix him some coffee, some bacon and eggs, and some biscuits with gravy. He was to sit down without the gun while she prepared him breakfast. He did. When the meal was ready, he sat down at the table, and after grace was said, began to eat. He told Louise that the breakfast was just like his grandmother used to make.

Someone apparently had seen the escaped inmate enter their house, and, soon after he finished breakfast, cars with police sirens began to approach and surround the house. The escapee shouted out that they had found him and he went for his gun. Louise stopped him, telling him that he did not need the gun. She instructed him to get behind her and for her husband to get behind the escapee. She indicated that together she and Nathan would walk him out the door, with her in front and her husband behind him, so that the police could not shoot. The escapee would then turn himself over to them peacefully. That's exactly what they did. The DeGraffenreids saved his life. One other inmate had escaped that same day but was killed when he resisted arrest.

This story embodies a Christian couple who confronted the powers of a man with a gun and the police. Louise crossed the wall between herself and the escapee and fixed him breakfast and obviously built a relationship of some trust with him in a very short time. When the police came, Louise and Nathan formed a protective shield with their own bodies between the escapee and the police. They stood on a wall between the powers. This is the embodiment of living into the reality of a new age; it is an act of new creation.[21]

In Paul's gospel God has set us free from the powers, and we are called to that freedom (Gal 5:13). It is a freedom empowered by the Spirit (2 Cor 3:17). It is a freedom where we are delivered from the powers of the flesh, from those corrupted and misplaced desires that hold us in bondage. We are

---

21. This story occurred in Mason, Tennessee, in 1984 and was carried by the national press. I was sent a copy of the story by Ken and Jean Kettlewell of New Concord, Ohio. It did not have publication data.

encouraged not to allow our flesh to become an occasion of self-indulgence (Gal 5:13-16). It is the freedom of a community where each person is provided with gifts to serve that community and to make their witness known (1 Cor 12). It is a freedom where Paul can become all things to all people for the sake of the gospel (1 Cor 9:22). It is a freedom where the church is called to be an alternative community, not to be conformed to this world but by presenting our bodies as a living sacrifice, we are to be transformed by the renewing of our minds (Rom 12:1-2).

And, yes, Paul does instruct slaves and others to remain in "whatever condition you were called." It seems clear that Paul believed the return of Christ was imminent (1 Cor 7:29-31). For that reason he encouraged this accommodative stance to slavery and suggested that "if you are actually able to be free, take advantage of the opportunity." But he also stated that "anyone who was a slave when they were called by the Lord has the status of being the Lord's free person" (1 Cor 7:21-24).

Cain Hope Felder in his commentary on Paul's letter to Philemon is instructive here. In this letter Paul is sending back Philemon's escaped slave, Onesimus. If one does a quick reading of this letter, it may seem to focus on slavery, observes Felder, but he maintains that "the central meaning and purpose" is rather to propose a quite new and different connection between Philemon and Onesimus, one based on the friendship each has with Paul and their membership in the church.

In Felder's perceptive study of this letter of Paul, he argues that we can find "clues" about Paul's stand on slavery. For example, Paul knew that there were provisions and sanctions for specific forms of slavery in the Hebrew Bible. There was also the "abhorrence of slavery" by the people of Israel after their enslaved sojourn in Egypt. Felder further claims that Paul was "astute" when he did not take on "the role of a pronounced abolitionist" given how "foolhardy for himself " it would have been in those times and how damaging it would have been to the young Christian movement. Given these difficult circumstances, Felder is astonished by Paul's statements in Galatians 5:1, 1 Corinthians 7:21, and 2 Corinthians 11:20-21. From these Pauline passages Felder concludes that Paul certainly was not a defender of slavery. "On the contrary, they reflect an attitude consistent with the appeal made in the letter to Philemon, making the words found there all the more poignant and significant."[22]

---

22. Felder, "The Letter to Philemon," 11:886. See also Martin, *Slavery as Salvation*, who delineates differences between American slavery and that of the ancient world.

These few comments do not exhaust the use of the word *freedom* in Paul's writings but do suggest that God's righteous act in Christ—God's putting things right, God's justice—is an act of deliverance, a setting free. Empowered by the Holy Spirit, this calling and inauguration of a new community is gifted with the resources and capabilities to live out a new reality. Indeed, "Christ has set us free for freedom" (Gal 5:1).

Mercy

The second characteristic of God's righteousness in God's act in Christ is that of mercy. Needless to say we are not used to thinking of mercy as a characteristic of justice. Typically it is seen as an exception to or a release from the claims of justice. There is an old story about a soldier who went AWOL from Napoleon's army. Subsequently caught, the soldier was convicted and condemned to die. His mother gained an audience with Napoleon and begged for his life. Napoleon stated that the soldier did not deserve mercy. The mother in response stated, "If he deserved it, it would not be mercy." Typically, the notion of justice as "getting what one deserves" runs long and deep in Christianity and Western culture. While I will not contend that getting what one deserves is unrelated to a Christian justice, I do want to suggest that mercy is intrinsic to Christian justice, especially when justice is understood in terms of God's righteousness. There is simply no way even to approach God's righteousness without attending to the massive role of mercy in divine rectification. I turn to four places in Paul to account for this claim of its intrinsic character in divine righteousness.

In Romans 3:21 Paul makes the daring proclamation that "but now God's righteousness has been revealed apart from the Law, which is confirmed by the Law and the Prophets." This assertion follows Romans 1:18–3:20, where Paul develops the argument for the guilt of all of humanity, first that of the pagan world and then that of the Jews. As he says then in 3:23, "All have sinned and fall short of God's glory." It is God's world-altering action, contrary to what humankind deserves, by which we are rectified by the faith of Christ.

Later, in Romans 5:10 we are told that "if we were reconciled to God through the death of his Son while we were still enemies, now that we have been reconciled, how much more certain is it that we will be saved by his life?" Mercy permeates the righteousness of God in Paul.

This theme of reconciliation is picked up again in the well-known passage of 2 Corinthians 5:16-21, which I will consider more fully below. Here I am specifically interested in verse 21 where it says, "God caused the one

17

who didn't know sin to be sin for our sake so that through him we could become the righteousness of God." In making Christ sin, God has subjected him to the powers, though Christ was innocent of sin. Nevertheless, Christ takes on the human condition, becoming subject to the powers of sin, death, and those elementary forces. My friend William B. McClain says this is "the God who gets with us in order to get to us." All of these actions express the mercy of God. God's right-making action, God's justice, in the world is one of mercy. This is the God who will not be God without us.

There are also those great chapters in Romans 9–11 where Paul struggles with the salvation of the Jews, of those under the law. Here he speaks that ringing word: "As by their [the Jews] disobedience we have received mercy; so by our disobedience they shall receive mercy" (11:31). It is God's mercy that saves those under the law and those of us who are not. Mercy is not an exception to God's righteousness; it participates directly and fully in God's saving action of setting things right. Mercy is a dimension of justice, not an exception to it, not some norm in tension with justice.

Finally, the extraordinary text in Philippians 2:4-6 proclaims the *kenosis* where Christ Jesus, though he was in the form of God, nevertheless does not regard himself equal to God or one who is to exploit that relationship. Rather, Christ empties himself and takes on the form of a slave, by becoming subject to the enslaving powers of the world. He humbles himself and becomes obedient to God even to the point of death on a cross. That is, he is made captive to those who demean and torture him, he is made a slave to death. "Therefore," says the text, "God highly honored him and gave him a name above all names, so that at the name of Jesus everyone in heaven, on earth, and under the earth might bow and every tongue confess that Jesus Christ is Lord, to the glory of God the Father" (Phil 2:9-11). In this text the humbling of Christ is a work of obedience to God not to pay for sins (in the plural) so that we may be forgiven but rather to take on and defeat sin and death as powers and in God's exaltation of Christ to make him Lord of the cosmos and victor over the powers.

Rodney Stark in his study of the growth of Christianity in the first three centuries of its existence reports the response of the church to two severe plagues that occurred in that time. When the plagues hit, a frightful populace left the cities for the small towns and rural areas. Even the great physician, Galen, went to his country estate during this time. The Christians, however, stayed and cared for the people who were ill with the plague. Stark states that all that most people needed in order to survive was someone to care for them. The people of Christian congregations served this purpose, and in the process brought many into the faith. Stark names this as one of the significant factors in the growth of the church in this time.

Another factor in church growth related to the practice of killing newborn baby girls because they were regarded as a financial handicap by their families. In contradistinction, boys were privileged because of the anticipated economic advantage they would bring to their parents in old age. Stark observes that, as a result of Christians saving daughters, the church wound up later with a surplus of young women of marriageable age who then practiced a form of marital evangelism when they were subsequently wedded to pagan young men![23]

In both cases, these practices by a community that saw itself as an alternative to the world embodied the character of mercy in their responses both to those who suffered from the plague, from dangerous practices of infanticide, and the devaluation of baby girls in that culture. This witness manifests the new creation in Paul's thought and speaks powerfully to it. These acts of mercy are not some norm in tension with justice but a fundamental expression of it when understood in terms of God's apocalyptic righteous act in Jesus Christ.

Reconciliation

I have already referred to 2 Corinthians 5:16-21, where Paul tells us that we have this ministry of reconciliation. He acknowledges that we once regarded Christ from a human point of view but that we no longer know him that way; indeed, we now regard no one from the human point of view. If we are in Christ, there is a new creation where everything has become new; the old has passed away. In this passage Paul is speaking from God's self-disclosure and God's change of history. It is God's act in Christ that has reconciled the world to God. People's trespasses are not to be held against them, and this message of reconciliation belongs to the church, that manifestation of new creation that God has established and empowered by the Spirit. We are now ambassadors for Christ calling people to be reconciled through the church.

The church as the new creation is the community called to tell the world that the walls no longer matter. The hostile divisions of the world have been decisively defeated and will ultimately be brought down. It is also a new reality into which we are called to live—to live in the world in ways where the walls do not matter to us. It is to live in the confidence that we

---

23. Stark, *The Rise of Christianity*, 76–94, 95–128.

can ignore the walls in some cases and in others stand against them. This opens up a new space in history, one where we are offered a new identity and empowered to live in a community dedicated to the unity won for us by Christ.

I think of Will Campbell in relation to a mission against the walls. His campus ministry at the University of Mississippi in the fifties and his work with the National Council Churches led him into a deep involvement in the civil rights movement. Campbell was the only white person present in the room when Martin Luther King Jr. began the Southern Christian Leadership Conference. In 1957 he walked with Elizabeth Eckford, one of the "Little Rock Nine," when those courageous African American youth integrated the Little Rock High School in Arkansas. His civil rights activity took him across the South to locations of protest and nonviolent action. He saw firsthand the suffocating oppression of the black community, and he stood against it.

Yet, as his ministry continued, he gave a significant amount of his time to imprisoned Ku Klux Klan members. For example, he visited Tommy Tarrants, a Klansman at Parchman Prison in Sunflower County, Mississippi. Tarrants, filled with hate and a terrorist, was a key figure in the Klan program of violence against blacks and their sympathizers even as a teenager. When Tarrants attempted to bomb the home of a progressive Jewish businessman, the FBI set a trap and shot and nearly killed him. His crime gained Tarrants a thirty-year prison sentence at Parchman Penitentiary. It was there that Campbell began to visit Tarrants and spent hours with him behind the barbed wire of Parchman. Campbell, joined by several others, took an active interest in Tarrants, and the Klansman began moving in a new direction. Eventually rejecting racism, he became a Christian and in time was paroled. He then entered the University of Mississippi, completed a degree, and responded to the call to be an evangelical minister. In speaking of his ministry among the Klan, Campbell put it quite simply "that Mr. Jesus died for the bigots as well."[24]

When God rectified the world, when God put things right in Christ, this divine act was an act of reconciliation, so that reconciliation as justice is utterly central to God's revelation, to God's Self-disclosure, and God's altering of history. This is why a Christian justice cannot be reduced simply to "getting what one deserves." This God who sets us free from the cosmic powers, who takes the form of a slave in mercy, who reconciles the world

---

24. Quoted in Frye Gaillard, "The Gospel according to Will," 2, 39, 163. I am indebted to Gaillard for this story about Campbell and Tarrants.

to Self in Christ reveals and manifests a justice in Jesus that is radically alternative to the justices of the world. I know of no other tradition that so describes justice in these terms. It is an important witness to embody and to live out in a society that conceives justice too narrowly as one of rights and of getting what one has coming.

A CONCLUDING NARRATIVE

On October 2, 2006, Charles Carl Roberts IV entered the one-room Nickel Mines school in the Old Order Amish Community in Bart Township, Lancaster County, Pennsylvania. After taking hostages and a standoff with police of less than an hour, Roberts shot ten girls ages six to thirteen. Five of them were killed. He then committed suicide.

The response of the Amish community to these killings embodies and performs a Christian justice of liberation, mercy, and reconciliation. It is a story of the church as new creation that can stand as a conclusion to this chapter.

During the standoff, one of the Amish girls begged Roberts to shoot her so that her sister could live. Later that same day one of the grandfathers of the girls who were killed urged some of his younger relatives not to hate Roberts and instructed them, "We must not think evil of this man." Yet another Amish father observed, "He had a mother and a wife and a soul and now he's standing before a just God."[25] Jack Meyer of the Brethren Community, a neighbor of the Amish people in Lancaster County, commented, "I don't think there's anybody here that wants to do anything but forgive and not only reach out to those who have suffered a loss in that way but to reach out to the family of the man who committed these acts."[26]

Within hours of the shooting an Amish neighbor visited the Roberts family and offered consolation and forgiveness. Another Amish man embraced Roberts's father for most of an hour in order to offer solace and sympathy. At the shooter's funeral thirty Amish people attended, and Marie

---

25. Daniel Burke, "Amish Search for Healing, Forgiveness after 'The Amish 9/11,'" *Religion News Service,* October 5, 2006. Archived from the original on October 21, 2006, http://web.archive.org/web/20061021051654/http://www.religionnews.com/ArticleofWeek100506.html.

26. "Amish grandfather: 'We must not think evil of this man,'" *CNN.* October 5, 2006. Archived from the original on December 10, 2007, http://web.archive.org/web/20071210073251/http://www.cnn.com/2006/US/10/04/amish.shooting/index.html.

Roberts, the shooter's widow, was one of those few outsiders invited to the service for one of the young murdered girls. Later, the Amish community set up a fund to help support the widow and her children.

In response to these and other offerings of love and comfort, Marie Roberts responded with these words in a letter to the Amish community: "Your love for our family has helped to provide the healing we so desperately need. Gifts you've given have touched our hearts in a way no words can describe. Your compassion has reached beyond our family, beyond our community, and is changing our world, and for this we sincerely thank you."[27]

A Christian justice of the kind embodied and carried out by this Amish community cannot simply be a matter of belief; it cannot be merely a position. It requires the formation of a just people, those who are rectified and shaped in a community where they embody and enact a justice of liberation, mercy, and reconciliation. This requires communal configuration in the sensibilities and dispositions that we bring to the world. We turn next to this important issue.

---

27. I am indebted here to the *Wikipedia* encylopedia. "West Nickel Mines School Shooting," accessed September 30, 2015, https://en.wikipedia.org/wiki /West_Nickel_Mines_School_shooting.

Chapter 2

THE FORMATION OF A JUST CHURCH

One of the hardest things to do in baseball as a catcher is to hold onto the ball when another player attempts to score at home plate and runs over you. Having caught for thirty-five years in amateur baseball and softball, I can testify to the difficulty of such skill. While I was never able to do it, I have seen catchers who nevertheless held onto the ball even when knocked unconscious. Obviously, the tendency is for the catcher to release the grip on the ball when a collision occurs between the catcher and another player running at full speed. Being able to hold onto the ball is something that has to be learned; one really has to be trained to do it.

One way to do this training is for someone to stand twenty or thirty feel away and to throw a soft toss to the catcher in training. Why a soft toss? Because a soft toss is harder to catch, especially with a catcher's mitt, and because you have to keep your eye on the ball. You have to watch the ball all the way into the glove and grip the ball once it is in the pocket of the mitt. While this is happening, someone else with a big pillow stands next to the catcher, and as soon as he catches the ball they slam the pillow into him, doing so as soon as possible after the ball is caught. This liturgy is repeated over and over many times across many days.

A practice like this is designed to keep the catcher's attention focused, first, on catching the ball—for example, not looking at the looming player coming down the base path and taking one's eye off the ball—and, second, to reverse the tendency to release one's grip on the ball when hit. Such training requires the development of sensibilities, the building of dispositions, the focus of concentration, the formation of skills, and a kind of courage that is built, at least in part, on the fact that a trained catcher is so engaged in the activity of getting the opposing player out that he or she does not have time for fear. Your focus is elsewhere.

With most congregations I find very little such training in the sensibilities, the dispositions, the sustained concentration, and the skills of a

Christian justice. There are exceptions, but this is not found in most Christian communities. To be sure, churches do worship and provide Christian education and many do practices of charity, and these are not to be negated, but I do not find much explicit training in a Christian justice of the kind laid out in the last chapter. For many, justice is reduced to studying social issues and having a point of view, a position on certain issues. When we do find those skilled and formed in a Christian justice, it usually occurs in the context of a long ministry in certain missional work where they have gained through intentional practice the requisites necessary for an embodied and communal justice.

The church is the new creation brought forth by God's rectifying act in Christ. With this Paul instructs us "because of God's mercies...present your bodies as a living sacrifice that is holy and pleasing to God." We are not to "be conformed to the patterns of this world, but be transformed by the renewing of [our] minds so that [we] can figure out what God's will is—what is good and pleasing and mature" (Rom 12:1-2). This transformation requires the formation of our very bodies and minds.

Anthropologist Talal Asad makes the case that a tradition is basically a performance, one in which we embody a tradition and one in which we enact, we perform that tradition. Following Marcel Mauss, he contends that the body is "our first and most natural instrument." That is, our work must be first on our bodies to teach, to train, to form them. Further, he suggests that the body is an assemblage of invited appetites, that is, that we invite into our bodies appetites that require formation.[1] If I want to live a healthy life in my older years, I must invite in good practices of exercise, nutrition, adequate sleep, and a good balance of work and leisure. Formation involves these kinds of invitations of appetites.

The Christian tradition requires the invitation of a number of appetites into the life of the church. I think of the worship of God who has set the world right in Christ, and the celebration of the future in the Eucharist where we embody the reality—though only fragmented and partial—that we are one, and that the walls are down. There can be a "thousand" times of fellowship where we can learn hospitality and community, where we practice forgiveness and healing and new life in the Spirit. Further, missional opportunities to engage people who are other offer important ways to shape our lives, and where we necessarily must shed our appetites of paternalism and one-way relationships of interaction. Worship, baptism, Eucharist, life

---

1. Asad, *Formations of the Secular*, 95, 251–56. Cf. David Scott and Charles Hirschkind, eds., *Powers of the Secular Modern*, 151–53, 234–35.

together, and outreach are the grounding of our tradition. These are the bases for a range of practices of the liberation, the mercy, and the reconciliation of a Christian justice. Crucial to this work is the formation of the senses.

FORMATION OF THE SENSES

Formation requires the shaping of the body. I think here especially of our sensibilities, that is, the senses by which we see, hear, smell, taste, and touch the world and others. Walter Ong calls this the sensorium, the organization of the senses. He finds that our senses are historically and culturally formed. People do not see, hear, taste, touch, and smell the world in the same ways.[2] The formation of our senses are specific to the times, the culture, and the form of life in which we live.

Seeing

German writer and statesman Johann Wolfgang von Goethe (1749–1832) believed that we can form our senses. He developed the concept to *behold* by which he meant the cultivation of the senses. The development of this capacity, he maintained, can transform the self. By the fashioning of new organs of perception, we build up our cognitive capacities and by this enhance our world.[3]

This is key in the formation of people for a Christian justice. I delivered a lecture to a national meeting of the Disciples of Christ in Indianapolis. As it happened, Mac Charles Jones, then pastor of St. Stephens Baptist Church in Kansas City, was invited to preach at a worship service for this meeting in a park in the center of the city. Mac preached a powerful sermon but also a long one. When he finished, he and I had thirty minutes to catch a flight at the airport that lay about twenty minutes away. We were hustling down this wide side walk headed for a waiting cab at the corner. As we were moving along, a homeless man headed directly toward us. He knew who we were.

"Pastors," he asked plaintively, "can you spare a little change for some food?"

I knew Mac had had a long history of working with homeless people, and I waited to see what he would do and I would follow suit. So I slowed down a half step. Mac seemed to speed up. He was a big man, over six feet tall and at least three hundred pounds. Wearing a rain coat, he raised his

---

2. Ong, *The Presence of the Word*, 190ff.
3. J. W. von Goethe, *Theory of Color in Scientific Studies*, 207–16, esp., 210-11.

arms as he moved toward the man to embrace him in a hug that virtually enveloped him.

"Brother," Mac answered, "yes, we have some money. But you need to eat, and we are going to take you to lunch. Come on and get in the cab with us."

I thought to myself, "Mac, we do not have time to take this man to lunch. We are going to miss our plane." But I said nothing to Mac.

When we got into the cab, Mac instructed the driver, "Mister, drive straight to the airport. The first time you see a fast food restaurant right on the street, stop, keep the meter running, and we will take this man in to buy him lunch. We will come out immediately and you can take us then to the airport, as quickly as you can."

That's exactly what we did. Mac and I put together twenty dollars, and Mac told the cashier, "Give this man whatever he wants to eat, make sure he eats it, and then give him the remaining cash."

I have thought about this event many times. I saw that man as an interference, someone who would make us miss our flight. Mac saw him as a brother, and it made all the difference in the world. Further, Mac was deeply experienced and trained in working with homeless people. Understanding the effects of consuming alcohol day after day without food, he read that situation exactly right. He knew the man needed to eat. He also knew that if there was cash waiting and dependent upon the homeless man finishing his lunch that he would indeed eat.

Notice here not only Mac seeing him as a brother but also his perceptual grasp of the wider circumstances of the man's need for food and the options available to make sure he got it. In sports we often talk about the capacity of a player in soccer or basketball having field or court vision or the capacity to take into account the range of circumstances around a player during the game. Exceptional players have that field or court vision. Mac had that. I simply never would have thought of putting the man in the cab and taking him to a fast food restaurant for lunch. That was so outside my experience and what I was trained to do that it would not have occurred to me. It embarrasses me to say that now, but it is true. By the way, we made it to the plane in plenty of time. They closed the door to the gangway immediately behind me as I followed Mac through the gate.

Hearing

The capacity to hear is also a learned practice, really an art. Often as clergy we are taught to listen with a "third ear," meaning to listen for what is going on with a person who comes to us for help. We are taught to listen to the presenting problem a person may bring for help, but it is crucial to hear what may be behind that, what may be the real issue. To be helpful, we must listen to the issue behind the problem the person initially tells us. I think here of a woman who comes in to talk about her prayer life but may need to address the issue of spousal abuse by her husband.

There is a range of such trained practices in justice work. Let me just name three here, and save other comments for later when I address listening more fully. First is the commitment to listening itself. This involves the willingness to devote time to "one-on-ones" with people and to meet them where they are. Second, it involves a skill in teasing out the stories of people to discover what seriously matters to them. The experience of organizing with which I am familiar is one in which story is the basic way to learn people's hurt, oppression, anger, passions, and loves. Third is the capacity to listen, to focus on the other person, to share appropriately; these are critical to the development of a relationship from which justice can be pursued. All of these are practices and skills to be learned and developed.

Smell

When I began thinking through the formation of the sensibilities, I was stuck on the issue of smell. I did remember asking my physician about how he dealt with smell on hospital wards. I told him that as a pastor I had trouble dealing with odor, especially where there were cancer patients. He told me that he had learned to "turn his nose off." I knew immediately that I did not yet have that skill.[4]

So when I began to work on the sensibilities for a lecture, I called my friend, John Flowers, who had had a very effective ministry with homeless people in San Antonio, Texas. I told John that I was having difficulty with the issue of smell in working with justice issues and asked if he had thought about and worked with the question. To my surprise, he answered immediately.

"Oh, sure, I had to develop that early on. I discovered that if a homeless person had hygiene issues, that is, smelled bad, that typically they had other issues as well, things like mental problems, dysfunctions, or some such thing. When I found homeless people who were more hygenic, I realized that they were probably pretty functional. What I learned from this

---

4. See Flower's and Vannoy's very helpful book on ministry with the poor, *Not a One Night Stand*, 20.

was that I could use smell as a diagnostic tool. It helped me to know what I needed to do to be helpful to the person. Smell helped me learn to respond differently to different people."

I was so impressed with his response that I asked if there was more.

"Well, yes, when I first moved to Travis Park Church, I was bothered by the fact that the alley of the church smelled like urine because the poor could not find another place to relieve themselves. After a time I began to understand this sacramentally. It meant that the church was important to the poor, that it was the place they hung out, that it was a central place for their very lives."

To smell urine sacramentally is a learned art and practice.

Taste

When I think of taste my mind turns inevitably, it seems, to the fourth beatitude in Matthew, where it reads, "Happy are people who are hungry and thirsty for righteousness, because they will be fed until they are full" (Matt 5:6). Of course, one usually reads hunger and thirst here as metaphors, certainly not an incorrect way to read the passage. At the same time, I find a relationship between this passage and the Eucharist that changes these terms from being only a metaphor.

I grew up in a Methodist church that practiced the Eucharist once a month. We used shot glasses and broken crackers. I was raised in a setting where we understood Holy Communion as a memorial service where we remembered Christ's final night before crucifixion. While I regarded the Lord's Supper as a sacred time, I must confess that I never found myself looking forward to it; neither did I find myself empty if I did not celebrate it on a given Sunday. Not only was it not that important to me, I did not desire it or yearn for it.

Later, I would be on the faculty of Saint Paul School of Theology where we celebrated the Eucharist each week and more. After that, I was part of the Asbury United Methodist Church in Phoenix, Arizona, where I participated in the Eucharist every Sunday. During those years at Saint Paul and later at Asbury I began to feel that my week had not been complete or right if I had not eaten the bread of life and drunk from the cup of salvation. I found myself looking forward to it and a sense of loss on those occasions when I missed the sacrament.

Something else happened as well. More and more I saw the Eucharist not only as a memorial service but a re-membering, a time when the members of the body of Christ came together so as to be that body. It became, moreover, a time when I appreciated the diversity that was represented by our school and later by the Phoenix congregation. These occasions gave me a sense of remembering the future—that is, a time when the unity of those gatherings became a foretaste of that great banquet of the reign of God that comes beyond history, when all people from all places and races and classes and conditions shall finally be one. The Eucharist became an embodiment of that reconciliation that God has brought in Jesus Christ.

Through these same years I found myself in eucharistic moments that marked me for life. I remember an evening with Will Campbell in his cabin down the path from the back of his house in Mt. Juliet, Tennessee, where he hosted a class of Saint Paul students, coinstructor Larry Hollon, and myself. He sang us country music songs with biting lyrics about social wrongs and human hopes for the better part of an hour, telling us that these songs could help us understand what theological education should be about. It has to be one of the finest hours of that kind I have ever known. When he stopped singing, he went to an old fashioned ice box—not a refrigerator—took out a Mason jar full of white lightening moonshine whiskey, raised it to bless it before the Lord, and then passed it around to all of us in celebration of the Eucharist.

In 1965 I was in the march from Selma to Montgomery that protested for voting rights for African Americans in Alabama and across the country. As we entered Montgomery on the last day, I was walking on the right side of the line of march when a black woman walked up to me with peanut-butter and jelly sandwiches in one hand and a plastic gallon jug of strawberry Kool-Aid in the other. She thrust those into my hands, and, looking at me, said, "Heah, brother, we gonna overcome!" With that she disappeared back into the crowd. As I took one of those sandwiches and handed the others to the person next to me, I could hear the words, "This is my body broken for you." As I took a drink from the jug and passed it on, I heard the words, "This is my blood, which is shed for you and for many."

I will never forget these moments and others of similar impact. They have forever bonded my understanding of the Eucharist and the hungering and thirsting after righteousness. By this strange "alchemy" of grace working through practice I find that my taste has changed, that the partaking of common elements of bread and juice have altered my very sensations of mouth and tongue. As Sara Miles observes, there is a hungering for food that goes beyond food. The infinite shows up in the finite.[5] There is a hungering and thirsting after righteousness.

5. Miles, *Take This Bread*, 23.

Touch

On the matter of the sensibilities, touch takes on critical importance, especially around the issue of observing boundaries and not overstepping them. There are far too many tragic consequences from people working for justice who did not maintain appropriate boundaries with other coworkers. These have often damaged, where they have not destroyed, the witness of significant actors in the quest for justice.

My great teacher was Walter G. Muelder, professor of social ethics and dean of the Boston University School of Theology while I was a student there. I shall never forget a lecture when he said, "If you intend to stay in the work of social justice and social action, you need to keep your hair combed, your face washed, and your pants zipped or up as the case may be." It was trenchant advice.

But I want to address other dimensions as well. Part of the way I use touch is metaphoric in the sense of doing things with the right touch, the right balance or approach. Touch here has to do with savior faire. It is related to that notion of know-how mentioned above. The right touch has a sense of timing, a sense of understanding the flow of an occasion or the sequence of events. It is composed, in part, of intuitive skills, of grasp. There is the element of "feel," an implicit knowing that can never be adequately described. There is a holistic character to touch, a capacity to grasp the gestalt of what is happening, and to respond appropriately to it.

Back in the sixties I was in an important meeting with the Boston School Committee, which had battled against integration of schools even though the Supreme Court decision of *Brown v. Topeka, Kansas, Board of Education*, outlawing segregated schools, had been made in 1954. One of the school committee members had made a speech obviously persuasive with the supporters of de facto segregation. He concluded that speech by shouting, "How can you put a black child of poverty and a white middle-class child together in the same classroom?"

The room fell silent for some five seconds, a long time. But then the voice of a civil rights organizer from the back of the room shouted in a voice weary with delay after delay and conveyed his exasperation with inaction, "Get two chairs!" The room irrupted in laughter. It devastated the temporary impact of the speech of the previous school committee member.

Still, I do not want to ignore the sensibility of touch itself, in the tactile sense of reaching out and laying hands on someone or shaking hands or patting someone on the shoulder, and so on. I interviewed Sam Mann, a white Alabaman, who served a black church in Kansas City for over forty years. When I asked him about touch, he went on a roll about issues like appropriateness and permission, but also about the central role of touch in healing, of the way Jesus touched people in making them well. He mentioned the touching and being touched involved in going to jail with people for a just cause, something he has done a good many times. Further, the place of touch in friendship, the energy stimulated by a touch of reconciliation, the importance of the commission of someone to a task and the role of laying on of hands, the part of touch in community, the place of appropriate hugging and of a holy kiss: all of these came out in his comments. "Justice is not something you say or describe; it is an act, it is what you do. Inevitably, it involves touch," he said. "To do justice, you have to be able to touch."

Mann reminded me of a handshake he does with Ajamu Webster, an engineer who is heavily involved in justice work with the African American community in Kansas City. When the two of them meet, each of them goes down on one knee, grabs the other's hand, hugs the other with the free hand, and then gets up with a bow. Mann understands this as a recognition of the other, of the strength of the other, as an affirmation of the worth and spirituality of the other, and as the embodiment of their solidarity.

It seems quite clear that the range of touch in the work of justice cannot be reduced to a few expressions but rather takes on a massive scope and vitality. Of course boundaries must be observed. The justice of touch is intrinsic to the touch of justice. And, of course, touch can become a ritualism. Yet, it is also a habitus, a way of living into an embodied justice, a performative enactment of the postures and physicalities of justice. The body is an instrument of justice, a key place for the formation of what God has set right.

DISPOSITIONS

The practice of formation, however, is not only one of transforming our senses but of shaping our dispositions as well. By dispositions I mean those characteristics built into us by the languages, concepts, practices, and training that have shaped the makeup of our identity, character, and operational inclinations and proclivities toward others and the world. I don't doubt that there are genetic, hormonal, and other physical attributes that play into the dispositions, but I want to look more at the role of socialization and training in the determination of these.

Methodist founder John Wesley called dispositions "tempers." These tempers could be sinful and evil or redemptive and good. He has one sermon where he preaches that fallen angels wage war against humanity. They close off the capacity of our hearts to see, stifle our love for God, and infest us with evil thoughts and tempers that continue to torment those they cannot destroy.[6] Yet, Wesley also believed that tempers could be sanctified and that from the tempers of sanctified persons came impulses that could change the wider society.[7]

I must confess that I am not sure about things like fallen angels; nevertheless, I am impressed with Wesley's relationships with the poor and his own tempers at work in ministry with them.[8] Manfred Marquardt, for example, underscores Wesley's approach to the poor as not a condescending charity, so typical of his time. Instead Wesley's social sensibilities and his tempers emerged from his solidarity with the people he served. It was out of this solidarity that Wesley and the Methodists of the eighteenth century responded to the challenges before them.[9] If this was not an adequate response, it may have been as full a response as was possible. It certainly cannot be dismissed, especially in the light of what others were doing.

Our dispositions are formed for the most part simply in the living of life. At the same time dispositions can be trained. This is indeed one of Wesley's contentions, that our tempers can be formed and transformed. I think here of dispositions around being nonviolent. In the civil rights movement demonstrators were often trained in remaining nonviolent even when subjected to severe verbal abuse and physical attack. Placing demonstrators in mock situations where sustained abuse was directed toward them was a way of building up a capacity to endure these attacks without returning the attacks in a reciprocally debasing or violent way. People were taught to lie on their backs when beaten and to cover their heads with their arms and to pull their knees up to their chests to protect more vulnerable parts of their bodies. When one person was being beaten, others were trained to throw their bodies onto the one being attacked to protect them, with yet others following suit in hopes that the attacker would tire and/or stop.

I know of not a single congregation that actually trains church members in nonviolent practices. With the level of violence in our communities, one would think that this would be an important set of skills to pursue. Such courses would certainly move from mere "head knowledge" and "know about" to "know how."

---

6. Wesley, "Sermon 72—Of Evil Angels."

7. Marquardt, *John Wesley's Social Ethics*, 136.

8. See my *The Future of John Wesley's Theology* for a fuller treatment of Wesley's theology and practice.

9. Marquardt, *John Wesley's Social Ethics*, 122-23.

I was lecturing on the East Coast and dealing with nonviolence as a practice. After the lecture ended, a young woman in her twenties came over to where I was and said, "Tex, I have been engaged in the training and practice of nonviolence for a number of years now. Last year, I was walking across my university campus in an isolated area where a good many shrubs lined the sidewalk. Suddenly, a man hidden in the shrubs jumped out, grabbed me, and dragged me back into them. He threw me down on the ground and began to tear away at my clothing. Struggling to resist nonviolently, I said to him, 'My name is Jane, what's yours? My name is Jane, what's yours?' But he kept tearing away at my clothing. Then I said, 'Can I take you to supper? I promise I will not call the police. Can I just take you to supper so we can talk?' Miraculously, he stopped. And that's exactly what we did. We talked and talked and we agreed to meet again the following evening. In fact, we met every day until I was able to talk him into a program dealing with his sexual violence that would hold him accountable. I simply want to say," she continued, "if it had not been for the training and the practice of nonviolence, there is no way that I would have known how to deal with him in that setting or had the courage to follow it up in order to help him."

It hardly needs to be said that his young woman dealt with a violent man in a way that was at least potentially liberating for him, demonstrated a massive mercy on her part, and apparently contributed to reconciliation not only between this man and her but, we hope, a reconciliation of the man with himself. At the time I was simply amazed at the sensibilities, the dispositions, and the skills she had displayed.

In this connection I think of Congressman John Lewis, who has the reputation of being the most physically beaten person in the history of the civil rights movement. Yet, he remained nonviolent. How he did so is revealed, at least in part, in a passage from his autobiography. An African American, Lewis had been raised in Alabama in poverty. He grew up on a farm in a house without indoor plumbing. With his family he rode six miles to church each Sunday on a wagon pulled by a mule. When he was six years old, he was put in charge of the chickens on the family farm. He writes of the chickens,

> They seemed so defenseless, so simple, so pure. There was a subtle grace and dignity in every movement they made, at least through my eyes.
> But no one else saw them that way. To my parents, brothers and sisters, the chickens were just about the lowest form of life on the farm—stupid, smelly nuisances, awkward, comical birds good for nothing but laying eggs and providing meat for the table.

Maybe it was their outcast status. The very fact that those chickens were so forsaken by everyone else, that drew me to them as well. ... I felt as if I had been trusted to care for God's chosen creatures.[10]

Lewis thinks that his concern and care for the chickens was the first indication of the man he would become, "what would come to shape my character and eventually guide me into the heart of the civil rights movement—qualities I certainly could not name at the time such as patience, compassion, nonviolence, civil disobedience, and not a little bit of willful stubbornness."[11]

To conclude, I began this chapter with the training of a baseball catcher to hold onto the ball after a collision with a player of the opposing team at home plate. I tried to suggest that we need exactly that kind of seriousness if we are to train people in the know-how of a Christian justice. I have further suggested that we pay far too little attention to the formation of a just church and a just people. The focus of this chapter has been especially oriented to the sensibilities and dispositions necessary for a just church as the new creation. Worship, Eucharist, prayer, and life together are all crucial in this formational work, to be sure. Still, we need to go further in the development of the sensibilities and dispositions of a Christian justice. And these will require specific practices, apprenticeship in the work of justice, and the settings, time, and training required. Of course, while transformed sensibilities and dispositions are necessary, they are not enough. We need, further, to be able to talk the talk and walk the walk of a Christian justice. We address these respectively in the next two chapters.

---

10. Lewis, *Walking with the Wind*, 24.
11. Ibid., 24–28.

Chapter 3

FLUENCY: TALKING THE TALK

When I was fourteen and in the eighth grade, I went out for the high school football team. We were basically cannon fodder for the B team. I began to have these pains in my lower back and down my legs. They grew worse as the days went on. One Saturday, I was home and the discomfort became so intolerable that I got down on the bathroom floor to try to ease the pain. I then found I could not get up. So I lay there for a couple of hours until my mother came home and helped me get to a bed. On the bathroom floor that afternoon, my mind came up with words and categories to account for the pain. I remember words like *paralyzed, incurable disease, dying,* the kinds of things that a fourteen-year-old might imagine. These concepts made the pain worse, it seemed, and added no little fear to the mix.

Mother took me to the orthopedist, who diagnosed me with spondylolisthesis, a condition in which one of my lumbar vertebrae had moved forward over the vertebrae below it and was out of place. The doctor prescribed an armchair back brace that went from my hips to just below my arms. I was to return to him that summer for surgery. He stated that I would be a semi-invalid for the rest of my life, though he thought that I might be able to play golf, depending on how the surgery went. I could never play football again, which I loved more than anything of that kind. As a result of my visit to the orthopedist, my language changed: *vertebrae out of place, brace, surgery, semi-invalid, life without football.* (I could not remember or pronounce the word *spondylolisthesis* for years.)

I never went back that summer. Instead, I went to a chiropractor who told me that I could manage the condition. I needed adjustments regularly, but I could live with the condition, even though I would always have the problem. And, yes, I had to give up football. While I was somewhat suspicious as to whether his treatments would work, nevertheless my words changed: *adjustments, manage the condition, live with the problem, no football.*

As the years went by, and it took a long time, I did continue to go to the chiropractor when I needed an adjustment, but my approach to my back changed as I learned more. I stretched my back and legs to prevent my hamstrings from getting tight. I learned that I had to stay in good condition so that my stomach muscles were strong and my belly relatively flat. I had to put a board under the mattress so my bed was flat and hard. I practiced the right way to lift objects. I also realized that when I would begin baseball season—which I played for a total of forty-five seasons—that I must stretch rigorously before and after I began doing wind sprints to condition my legs.

I have lived with spondylolisthesis—yes, I can now spell and pronounce the word—for sixty-six years. I am now relatively pain free. Sometimes I am stiff and occasionally have spasms, but I have learned to deal with them, sometimes with chiropractic care but mainly with conditioning, stretching, and proper lifting techniques. While this may not work for everyone (check with your medical team) it works for me.

The reason I try your patience with this example is to call attention to the changes in my language for this back condition and how it changed my experience and my practices. Note the difference in my language from that of a terrified fourteen-year-old to where I am today.

14-year-old	Orthopedist	Chiropractor	Today
Paralyzed	Brace	Adjustments	Conditioning
Incurable disease	Surgery	Live with the problem	Stretching
Dying	Semi-invalid	Manage the condition	Proper lifting
	No football	No football	Occasional chiropractic care

My point is that, as my language changed, my practices did too. I say this to emphasize the important role that language plays in our practices and experience. I am not suggesting that all one has to do is change one's language. My point, rather, is the importance of language and of how it shapes our experience. We do not have language without practices, and we do not have practices without language. Language itself is a practice and is embedded in yet other practices.

One thing more: Stanley Hauerwas points out that we do not transcend language in order to examine it. We continue to use language to study language.[1] The idea of somehow "getting above talk" or addressing "things we don't have words for" are incorrect descriptions of these efforts. There is no wordless or concept-less experience.

To be sure, we need to distinguish representative from nonrepresentative language. The former is language with which we attempt to describe something as carefully as we can; the latter points to or references something we cannot describe, such as a sunset. Yet, we still use language such as "it is beyond words." Indeed, there are many things we cannot adequately describe—perhaps everything is ultimately of this sort, a topic for another time—but the nonrepresentative language is still there.

WORD, CONCEPT, AND EXPERIENCE

Let me put it this way: our words, concepts, and beliefs shape our experience. If you change your language, you change your experience. Yes, I do continue to have back pain from time to time, but my experience with it is radically different than the way it used to be. I can have a spasm as bad as the one I had as a fourteen-year-old, though I hardly ever do, but it does not hurt the same, and I never get in a place like that time on the bathroom floor. I understand that the back pain can be relieved; I realize I can handle it; I know things to do. All these words, concepts, beliefs, and practices change the character of the pain.

Let me make the point even more sharply. If we do not have language for something, if we do not have a concept for something, it will not exist for us. I mean this in the sense of an observation by New Testament scholar Kenneth Bailey, who spent many years in the Middle East. He reports that sarcasm is a non-Middle Eastern form of speech, that there is not an equivalent word for sarcasm in Arabic. As a result he has spent hours of conversation in the Middle East trying to explain the word, basically to no avail.[2]

---

1. Hauerwas, *Working with Words*, 103.
2. Bailey, *Poet and Peasant*, 198–244.

THE IMPORTANCE OF TALKING THE TALK

I am making a point of this because of the way that talking the talk is dismissed in so many settings where I find myself, especially around justice work. I hear people say, "You can't just talk the talk, you've got to walk the walk." Well, of course, we must walk the walk, but that way of putting it diminishes the importance of talking the talk. Justice work that ignores talking the talk or pays too little attention to its important role makes a big mistake.

Part of the problem has to do with the way language is seen. We often think that language is merely a medium for our more real practices and lives. Philosopher James Edwards argues instead that language is "the stuff" of our lives, "the thread out of which all our patterns of thought and action are woven."[3] It is not mere "talk," it cannot be reduced to a mere medium. To treat it as such is to misplace a basic dimension of life, to ignore fundamental stuff.

When people are accused of not walking the talk—that is, not doing the things they say they believe—my suggestion is that we examine the practices in which such talk is embedded. We will have then far more descriptive power to bring to bear on such discrepancies. For example, the practices I see most active in people who do not walk the talk is that they have "a position" on social issues and that they "defend" their point of view with others with whom they come in contact. At the same time they are typically not engaged in active justice work, at least not that beyond talk.

Closely related to this is the kind of liberal for whom talking the talk is a form of status politics. That is, many people with liberal politics are in jobs and positions that do not pay top dollar. Big business people and certain other professionals make big money and are typically conservative. Liberals tend to inhabit positions that pay less. In this sense being a liberal and certainly a left winger does not provide big dividends for most. It usually does not pay off materially; the "scratch" is not there. Having a position on social issues, seeing oneself as prophetic, putting on a "hair shirt" metaphorically speaking, seeing oneself as a "public intellectual" can provide status. So talking the talk becomes a hungering and thirsting after status. No wonder it takes on a compulsive character that makes others hate us so.

Naming and identifying these practices of talking the talk associated with status politics is a far more penetrating critique. It does a helluva job on the status seeking. Understood this way, the role of language as the stuff

---

3. Edwards, *The Authority of Language*, 211.

of life is not diminished; it is seen rather as a powerful form of status politics. Not very admirable to be sure, but powerful.

VOCABULARIES AND RELIGION

To continue the point of the importance of words, concepts, and talking the talk, I turn to the work of William Greenway and Lee A. Wetherbee. They lift up the role of different vocabularies and the multiplicity of vocabularies in a given language. On their account, neutral or objective vocabularies do not exist. This does not mean that every particular use of language has an ax to grind. It does suggest that vocabularies come out of a form of life and that the particular expressions of that language are shaped by that form of life.[4]

An example, for three seasons I caught fast pitch softball for the Twin Cities Softball Team, an all-black team, except for me. (They could not find an African American dumb enough to catch, and I could not run fast enough to play anywhere else.) At practice sessions even before my first game with the club, I heard an expression I had never heard before, and I had been playing baseball and softball for more than thirty years at the time. If a player made a good catch, or fielded a ground ball well, or hit the ball sharply, the other players would shout out, "Hey, baby, I see you, man, I see you!" It struck me as very strange. I began to pay close attention to the use of the phrase. One thing eventually became clear to me about what was going on. Black guys had been making plays since the game began. The question was always whether anyone else saw it in a racist world. To tell another player that he is seen, that his play is noticed and acknowledged is a way to counter the ways that African American players have been ignored. Such uses of vocabulary, specific to the black community, cannot be reduced to having an ax to grind but certainly come out of a form of life that must be grasped if one is to engage the people of that group with some understanding.

Greenway and Wetherbee observe that "vocabularies speak themselves through us before we speak them," and as a result, they profoundly influence and constrain how we feel and think.[5] To illustrate this, I turn to Talal Asad's discussion of religion and its emergence in the modern period. The word *religion* did not exist in medieval times. The word in use then was *religious*, indicating that one belonged to a Catholic order. The concept of

---

4. Greenway and Wetherbee, "Vocabularies Matter," 1–9.
5. Ibid.

religion arrives on the scene in the discourse around the rise of the nation state. Asad makes the point that a major consequence of this new concept of religion was to separate faith traditions from the domain of power. A first step in this separation of religion was to give religion an essence, a universal one. This way, religion is seen as the genus and the various traditions of faith are understood as species of this "universal essence." Meanwhile, a number of moves were made to give this notion of religion certain categories for describing it. One of the first of these moves was to define religion as a matter of *beliefs*. It was also *subjectivized*, suggesting that it had to do with one's "innards," that is, one's subjective states like feelings and the subjective character of beliefs. Another move was then to see religion as peripheral and private, thus moving it out of the public square of social life. In the midst of all this, religion was conceived as an individual matter and to be elected by choice.[6] So note that the key terms or vocabulary for talking/writing about religion were the following:

- A universal essence
- A genus with faith traditions understood as species of this
- Beliefs
- Subjective
- Peripheral
- Private
- Individual
- Choice

I suggest that this is a, if not the, dominant way that religion is understood and the concept used in the United States. I say this even though we often hear now the distinction between religion and spirituality. My point is that this conceptualization of religion underlies both. We hear it in dozens of ways when people say things like, "My religion is a private matter just between God and me," and "I don't go to church but I believe in Jesus; that's all that matters." Or, "Religion ought not get into politics; it needs to serve the individual and the family"; "I have Jesus in my heart, that's what's important"; and the comments I mentioned earlier, "All faiths are equally true," or "We are all traveling up the same mountain, just by different

---

6. Asad, *Genealogies of Religion*, 28-54, especially 43-54. See also Scott and Hirschkind, eds., *Powers of the Secular Modern*, 287-88.

routes," suggesting religion as a genus and faith traditions as species of the same reality. And, "My faith is my own business, and I can choose whatever I want." I could go on and on. These kinds of statements remind me of the self-chosen journey of some lone wolf, out on the edges of life, looking for spiritual experience that fills a supposed need for self-fulfillment that confirms "who I am."

It is amazing how well such views of religion and spirituality fit in with a consumerist and rapacious capitalism and the discourse of the nation state. How convenient that it keeps one so comfortably within lifestyle enclaves living out a politics of identity that requires little communal, embodied, and disciplined resistance and challenge to the principalities and powers. These accommodative bourgeois machinations could hardly have been better planned by a brilliant conspiracy of power elites, and yet they operate as rather normal. It was Foucault who maintained that the primary form of domination was normalcy.[7]

As a Christian I cannot help but compare these kinds of assertions with the gospel of Paul where God has disclosed Self and changed history, where God has called out a new creation, and where ultimately God will destroy every ruler, authority, and power (1 Cor 15:24). Or, I think of other places in scripture where the nations rise and fall and are described as but a drop from a bucket (Isa 40:15). And, yes, Jesus's teaching of the centrality of the Rule of God and that we are to love God with all our heart, soul, mind, and strength.

Please understand, it is no wish of mine to get official prayers into the public schools or to put the Ten Commandments up on the walls of some government building. Such cozy relations between the church and the state deeply threaten the faith with an accommodation to the latter that not only mires the church in unjustifiable compromises with politicians and political authorities but moves the church into wayward and destructive idolatries. I will suggest below directions for the church's engagement in political and economic life that can resist faithless compromises with the state and the economic order but that nevertheless engage the public square.

FLUENCY

So given the importance of language as the very stuff of our lives and the ways in which the domination of the powers is secured, what is the work

---

7. Foucault, *Power/Knowledge*, 106–8.

of those who pursue a Christian justice, that is, how do we talk the talk? I love the notion of fluency as Talal Asad describes it, as "apt utterance and behavior," suggesting by this the capacity to use the language of a form of life.[8] Someone with fluency not only knows the right words to say but knows the right relationships of those words to each other—not only that, but also can work with inflection, with nuance, and a certain "musicality." My wonderful Old Testament professor, Harrell Beck, told the story of Mark Twain cutting himself shaving one morning and cursing a blue streak. His wife, unappreciative of such language and loss of control, walked over to where Twain was and repeated every word of his cursing outburst. Beck surmises that Twain was still enough of a nineteenth-century chauvinist to be taken aback by this unusual language from his spouse, but upon recovering quickly responded, "My dear, you've got all the words right, but you don't know the tune."[9]

The metaphor of musicality points to the complexities of fluency and the difficulties of developing the skills to move competently with language in a form of life. The complexities of fluency raise sharp questions with those who imagine that being able to get something said, with some descriptive accuracy, will communicate with a given group of citizens. Learning to talk the talk with a race or class or gender or orientation, for example, is a challenge that needs to be appreciated.

I can mention just three of these complexities of language here, but they, of course, are not exhaustive. The first has to do with the relationship of language to the sensibilities of a people. Harry Matthews is an American novelist who has now lived in France for many years. Although fluent in French he nevertheless writes in English. When asked why he does not write in French, his answer is that he did not attend high school in France and did not develop "the sensible infrastructure" of that kind of experience.[10] I understand this to mean that he did not develop the undergirding framework or features of the sensibilities of a developing teenager in France; he senses that he does not have the capacity to appreciate and to write out of the emotional or aesthetic ethos of the French people.

A second complexity is that the same word or phrase can be used in so many different ways. To know how a given expression is being used requires attention to the setting, tone of voice, inflections, gestures, knowing

---

8. Asad, *Genealogies of Religion*, 65.

9. David Felten has put together a collection of Beck's lectures and sermons. It is available on the website http://www.harrellbeck.com.

10. Bernard Flynn, "Maurice Merleau Ponty, *The Stanford Encyclopedia of Philosophy* (Fall 2011 edition), ed. Edward N. Zalta, http://plato.stanford.edu/archives/fall2011/entries/merleau-ponty/. See section 7, "Ontology of the Flesh."

glances, and so on. I am a Mississippian, and I have a close relative who is an extraordinarily fluent person in the idiom and dialect of Southern speech. I marvel at her capacity, for example, to use the phrase "bless her heart" or "bless his heart." Having heard her use this phrase hundreds of times across the years, I have come to realize that the phrase can mean anything from genuinely wishing for someone to be blessed to suggesting that the person in question simply go to hell.

The third complexity is what Paul Griffiths calls "deep grammar," by which he means the use of "central semantic terms" in a language and their "ordinary syntactical relationships."[11] Let me put it this way: What are the key words, concepts, and beliefs in use in the vocabulary of a given group? Further, what is the common or conventional relationships of these words, concepts, and beliefs to each other? Syntax, of course, has to do with the set of rules, principles, and processes that determine the structure of words and sentences in a language. But these rules and so forth are usually only implicitly understood and not articulated by the great majority of people who use them all the time. They just know when someone "doesn't sound right."

These few characteristics, of course, do not fully describe the complexities of language use so much as point to them. I am ever struck by the Gospel of John where the author proclaims that the Word became flesh. This is a rich claim in the Gospel, and my reading of it understands that phrase to mean not only that Christ became human but also that the Word takes on life among a people. I love, for example, the fact that Jesus's language was an idiom, Aramaic, and the phrase "lived among us" speaks to the significance of Jesus taking up residence in a particular culture. The Greek word that is translated as "lived" or "dwelled among us" is *skeenoo*, which means "pitched tent" or "tabernacled with us." It is this kind of enfleshed living with us that the Word entails. This is my way of indicating how important talking the talk finally is. For those interested in the work of a Christian justice, fluency involves this kind of embodied living with the language of a people and joining those linguistic practices in all their musicality, sensibilities, nuanced usage, and deep grammar.

I do not mean that a Christian justice simply accepts a language whole cart. Language is also an arena where the work of the powers is clearly displayed, and this work is to be resisted and challenged. For this reason the pursuit of justice requires reinterpretation and change in the language of a people.

---

11. Griffiths, "Witness and Conviction in *With the Grain of the Universe*," 70.

In a study of Abraham Lincoln's Gettysburg Address, Garry Wills observes that, while this speech made appropriate tribute to those killed in the battle and the larger war, Lincoln authoritatively named the purposes for which the United States was begun. Yet, Wills argues that Lincoln also called the nation to "a new birth of freedom" and voiced the dream of the country's founders who had established "a new nation . . . dedicated to the proposition that all men are created equal."

Wills contends that Lincoln voiced a new vision of the ideals of the nation and summoned the country to a new political identity by way of a new interpretation of its founding document. Wills comments that Lincoln takes on "the infected atmosphere of American history itself, tainted with official sins and inherited guilt." Lincoln sought to "cleanse the Constitution" with its acceptance of slavery not by destroying the document but by changing it from within. Lincoln moved from the letter of the document to its spirit, indicting its "legal compromise" with slavery. Wills comments,

> By implicitly doing this, he performed one of the most daring acts of open-air sleight of hand ever witnessed by the unsuspecting. Everyone in that vast throng of thousands was having his or her intellectual pocket picked. The crowd departed with a new thing in its ideological luggage, the new Constitution Lincoln had substituted for the one they had brought with them there. They walked off from those curving graves on the hillside, under a changed sky, into a different America. Lincoln had revolutionized the Revolution, giving people a new past to live with that would change their future indefinitely.[12]

I must say that I can appreciate the way in which Lincoln made an exquisite use of language in challenging and rereading the Constitution with a compelling new vision without finding Wills's statement that Lincoln had "revolutionized the Revolution" adequately credible. Here we are a century and a half later and that revolution has not yet occurred. We still live between the times; these powers have not been finally defeated in this ongoing American dilemma.

SO WHAT?

So where do these few comments about fluency take us in the quest for justice? What are some of the implications for the church as new creation?

---

12. Garry Wills, *Lincoln at Gettysburg*. Quoted in Hays, "The Liberation of Israel in Luke-Acts," 101–102.

What does it mean to commit to a justice of liberation, mercy, and reconciliation when it comes to talking the talk? Let me suggest some directions, albeit, again, not exhaustive.

A first step in fluency is to introduce into the linguistic fray of the powers a language of faith and faithfulness. I have already mentioned the inadequacy of a justice of rights and the importance of a Christian justice wherein we speak out of that distinctive voice not only to counter the limitations of rights language taken alone but also because this is the place of a more faithful response and greater conviction. Further, I will provide in a later chapter an account of a justice of the common good, which seeks alliance with those of other traditions.

1. To Address the Dearth of Language for the Communication of Faith and Spirituality

At this point, however, of examining the implications of a commitment to fluency, it is crucial to address what seems to be a dearth of language for communicating faith or spirituality. I was struck some years ago (in 1999) when sociologist Wade Clark Roof found that mainstream baby boomers "lack[ed] a clear and compelling religious vocabulary."[13] Later in 2011 sociologists Christian Smith and his associates in *their longitudinal study of young adults* found that 91 percent of their subjects held outlooks represented by "the dominant cultural paradigm of liberal individualism."[14] This liberal individualism is characterized by three assumptions:

> The first is that everyone, including the rich, has fairly earned their money through hard work. The second is that no person or society has the right to impose any external restrictions on any other individual. And the third is that people are naturally driven by self-interested acquisitive motives, which ultimately cannot be denied or deterred.[15]

Smith and associates describe these young adults as "consumed with consumerism."[16] They report a disturbing civic and political disengagement by these same young adults: a majority of 69 percent told the researchers

---

13. Roof, *Spiritual Marketplace*, 195, but see 191–203.
14. Christian Smith, Kari Christoffersen, Hilary Davidson, Patricia Snell Herzog, *Lost in Transition: The Dark Side of Emerging Adulthood*, 80.
15. Ibid.
16. Ibid., 108.

that "they were not political in anyway."[17] Further, they were not engaged in volunteer activity or charitable giving.[18] In response to the hope of many that this generation might bring a new day of active civic life and renewed political involvement, the findings of Smith and associates indicate that "such hopes have little basis in fact."[19]

In their account of the reasons for this disturbing state of young adult life, Smith and associates assert that what is "profoundly at issue" are the actual visions these young people have of "a human self and society" and what these "ought to look like." The basic problem is the way in which "the ideology and practice of mass consumerism" has constituted their identity and their visions of themselves. They are not "active citizens but acquisitive consumers."[20]

The findings of Roof on the lack of compelling faith vocabularies in baby boomers and the liberal individualism of these young adults offer powerful evidence of the importance of talking the talk. (I turn to the matter of practices in the next chapter.) In my reading of these two significant research programs, I am struck again and again with how much importance is given, especially, to individual "experience." So much of what these generations believe is pervasively based in their "experience," typically of a more consumerist kind. One's individual experience is used to counter tradition and to counter obligations that are seen as "external" to their lives. They seem to miss completely any discourse or sensitivity about *how mediated our experience is.* Experience is generated, shaped, and made an object of our knowing through the use of words, concepts, and beliefs operative in our forms of life.

This all says to me that we need a full-scale critique of these "spiritualities" and consumerist formations of experience. I find the best way to do this is through an analysis of the language and the offering of an alternative set of words, concepts, and beliefs. During 2014 I participated in an event we described as "a no-holds-barred theological conversation." The event occurred at the Midtown Arts Bar in Kansas City, Missouri. While it only went on for about four months, and we met only twice a month, I found more than a little openness to language analysis, especially as it related to issues of faith and spirituality. This brief exercise convinced me that a good deal more could be done in this regard.

---

17. Ibid., 196.
18. Ibid., 210–13.
19. Ibid., 212–13.
20. Ibid., 217.

My experience there fit very well with the observation of an unpublished paper by historian Ann Taves in which she discusses the kind of vocabulary that can unite "progressive Catholics and mainline Protestants." She reports very positive responses to the language of "Christian spirituality." The concept seems able to keep "a variety of conflicting connotations in tension":

1. "tradition and depth" with "ecumenical and inter-religious openness," and "institutional renewal and reform";

2. "corporate belief and practice" with "the immediate and explicit experience of the individual";

3. "the contemplating prayer of the monastery with committed action in the world";

4. with Catholics Christian spirituality underscores "the spiritual equality of the people of God, regardless of vocation";

5. and liberal Protestants find "an escape from the narrow confines of the piety of Protestant Evangelicalism."[21]

My use of these thoughtful observations by Taves would mainly require more explicit attention to the concrete practices of both discourse and other material practices in addressing faith. A person in our group one night argued that he was a free thinker and rejected all creeds. Another person in the group pointed out that freethinking had been a tradition since at least the seventeenth century, and, further, that there is no creed grander then the creed not to have one. This observation by an especially perspicacious young adult made not only for a significant conversation but took us into an arena not visited by most of those in the group. No one operates outside a tradition.

2. The Invention of New Language

A second implication is closely related to the first in that it involves the "invention" of new language. We need new words, concepts, and beliefs in order to resist the powers of this age. These new forms of language can

---

21. An unpublished paper from a conference on Catholic and mainline Protestant spirituality presented at the University of California in Santa Barbara, March 6–7, 1998. I am indebted to Roof, *Spiritual Marketplace*, 203, for this reference.

challenge established arrangements of power, open up contact with new experience, take people out of old categories, introduce people into new relationships, and engage them in new practices, and alternative forms of life.

Maggy Barankitse, born near Ruyigi, was caught up in the Burundi Civil War (1993–2004), which cost the lives of two hundred thousand members of the Burundi populace. Twice she escaped massacres in two villages where she was living along with her Hutu and Tutsi adopted children, who came from the conflicting ethnic tribes of the war. Maggy mothered her children and developed a ministry out of her call from God and her belief that the image of God in people is more important than their tribal identities. She played a key leadership role in the building of a village in Ruyigi on her own parents' land for children orphaned by the war. The village grew from twenty-five children, to one hundred, to five hundred, and then to more than ten thousand. She set up houses for the children to live together as families and organized businesses: a salon, a tailor and seamstress shop, a school for auto mechanics, a library, a tailoring school, language classes, and a computer school. She built a motion picture theater and a swimming pool, the latter because she wanted the children to be "immersed in a joy filled imagination."[22] Later, there would be four more children's villages and a center in Bujumbura, the nation's capital, with thirty thousand children served either directly or indirectly by this project.[23]

When it came time to name this alternative village, Maggy reports that they had to invent new language. Maggi and the children did not want to use the Kirundi word for peace, *amahora*. This was the word used by the warring tribes as they killed the parents of the children; the combatants had apparently taken the lives of villagers in the name of *amahora*. By naming the place Maison Shalom, Maggy and the children opened up a new form of life in that world and, I would say in Paul's terms, a new creation. Maggi denies that Maison Shalom is an orphanage that offers "services" to the children; it is rather a place of home and family, "God's family: princes and princesses, all destined to live in peace." I am struck by how central *call* is in Maggy's language, that she felt called to a mission, a mission based in God's love. In this new relation to God, she reports that "God liberated her from

22. Gregory Jones, "Maison Shalom." See christiancentury.org.

23. My summary of Barankitse's work comes from Emmanuel Katongole, *The Sacrifice of Africa*, 169–74, except for the brief quote from Jones, which is footnoted immediately above. The source for Katongole's description is Christel Martin, *La haine n'aura pas le dernier mot: Maggy la femme aux 10000 enfants*, unpublished translation by Trent Dailey-Chwalibog and David Dimas. Also note material from Bujumbura interviews, 170.

fear" and "raised her beyond herself to a new place and a new story into which she now wished to invite others."[24]

I know of no more embodied example of a Christian justice, one of liberation, mercy, and reconciliation, than Maison Shalom. Maggi saw how African language and practices of "community and solidarity" had been corrupted by "hatred and revenge"—a vivid and wicked enslavement by the principalities and powers. Maggy's mission became one of healing, not "simply one of advocacy to stop the killing," not even of mere "reconciliation between the ethnic groups." She said, "We need to create a system in which the hatred, however ferocious, no longer exists. We need to invent a way of living without hate."[25]

Maggy brought a new language to her mission. She maintains that all people are made in the image of God and therefore the identity of the Burundi people, indeed of all people, is love. Further, love is the human vocation: "We are created out of love and to love."[26] She sought "the seed for a new culture," "a new future," the rising up of "a new generation who will carry the light of love and forgiveness to all the surrounding hills."[27] Maggy says "love has made me an inventor."[28]

3. To Undermine a Dominant Fluency

A third implication of the need for a new fluency is to undermine the dominant fluency of the principalities and powers. This begins with the recognition and naming of the imperialism of the dominant categories and the offering of either new words, as we saw in the section above, or the reinterpretation of words in use. I will focus here on the latter. I find that placing a dominant word, for example, in a new context can be a highly effective way to make its dominant use anemic and provide a more compelling usage.

Let's take another look at the word *experience*. In the consumer lexicon the word often signifies a commodity, that is, we are offered experiences by being sold some new outfit, food, drink, car, furniture, vacation, home, investment, and so forth. We are not only subjected to thousands of advertisements but we are also exposed continually to commodity language in the practices of shopping, purchase, and then of living with the items and the

---

24. Kantangole, *The Sacrifice of Africa*, 172.

25. Ibid., 175.

26. Speech at the 49th international Eucharistic Congress, Québec, Canada, June 21, 2008, http://www.ecdq.tv/en/videos/.

27. Martin, *La haime*, 149, quoted in Kanangole, *The Sacrifice*, 176.

28. Katangole, *The Sacrifice*, 178.

experiences we have of them. I confess that I find myself craving for certain items and the experience of possessing them. I remember how much I was helped the first time someone named the fact that I was being sold an experience. The very naming of an obvious advertising practice and of my own response to it helped me alter my practices in relationship to advertising.

Further, I was helped even more, especially with the word *experience*, when Stanley Hauerwas offered that those of us caught in a consumerist world would do well to change the way we use that word. He suggested that we begin to think of experience as the word is used in a trade, that is, the kind of experience one builds up by learning the language of a craft and continually working in the array of practices associated with that kind of endeavor.[29]

I have done handyman chores around our home throughout my adult years. It frustrates me that I so often do something for the first time and therefore do not develop the background and skill so necessary to be competent at the work. I also find myself not knowing the right words to describe adequately a given project with its parts, sometimes the special tools required, and the associated framework in which my clumsy labor proceeds. On occasion, when I run into a situation I am not able to repair—say an issue with pipes or drainage, and the like—I call my plumber. I am always amazed at his capacity to size up and diagnose the predicament, at the economy of language he knows to explain the matter, at the relaxed and almost casual manner of his adept repair of the broken or worn out or plugged pipes, and then—to my mixed reaction of both awe and disgust—at his capacity to stay clean!

When *consumerist experience* is juxtaposed with the experience of a trade, the commodity form comes off quite weak in comparison. The word undergoes a transformation. It is precisely these kinds of practices around the language of domination that calls them into question and offers up a new or reinterpreted vocabulary to resist the words and concepts that capture us and cast us in the captivities of the dominant normalcy.

4. To Take People Out of Categories

Challenging the categories of the dominant discourse is crucial, and one of the best ways to do that is to take people out of categories. We have seen this in a rich number of ways in our lifetime. For example, the ways

---

29. Hauerwas, "Discipleship as a Craft, Church as a Disciplined Community," 881–84.

that people of color have taken on new language to challenge the dominant culture is a powerful example. Or I think of LGBTQ people and the acceptance of the word *queer* and the use of it in alternative, constructive, and positive ways. In this case it is a matter not of changing the term but of reconstituting its meaning and use.

Another example. In Kansas City I am fortunate to be a member of the Urban Summit, an organization of black political, business, nonprofit, and church leaders headed by Bishop James Tindall. In a presentation to the group, Melissa Robinson, the executive of the Black Health Care Association, spoke about the language and practices of her organization. She stated emphatically that they had stopped asking the question of clients, "What's wrong with you?" or in staff sessions, "What's wrong with her or him?" She indicates that this plays into old categories, which have no positive role in their diagnosis and treatment. Instead, in her agency they ask the question, "What happened to you?" According to her, this different question has brought a remarkable change in approach, one that takes people out of categories and offers a far more positive direction for assistance and treatment.

Another example: In a fascinating article on abortion and homosexuality Wendell Berry describes "categorical condemnation" as "the lowest form of hatred." "Cold hearted" and "abstract," categorical condemnation does not even have the heat or the courage hatred takes in its personal forms. It is mob hatred where cowards become brave and violent. Berry claims that the violence of a mob only takes hold after "a categorical refusal of kindness" to those who are other than we are. Observing that kindness does not have much currency in today's political and religious discourse, he asserts that the word is rich and necessary, "that we cannot live without it." Further, kindness connects with other words like *kin* and *nature*, and in the medieval world "*kind* and *nature* were synonyms," he reports.

In this discussion of kindness and its relationship to homosexual marriage, Berry acknowledges that his "faith and hope" reside in "the mercy of Christ, not in the judgment of Christians." He points to the scripture in the Gospel of John (8:1-11) where Jesus saves the woman caught in adultery from certain death. He does so by taking her out of the category where the accusatory mob cast her and locates her instead in Jesus's own kindness. Then, in a reversal, he puts her in the kindness of the mob itself by suggesting that only the sinless could throw the first stone. Defeated by this kindness, the mob leaves without further comment.

When Jesus asks the woman where those are who accuse and condemn her, she answers there is no one to do so. With that Jesus declares, "Neither do I condemn you: go and sin no more." Berry suspects that with Jesus's sense of humor, we may suppose that a smile crossed his countenance, especially since he knew the massive range of human sin and the limitless human vulnerability to it.[30]

5. To People the Minds of the Church

Certainly, moving people out of categories of captivity is crucial work. It is also important in talking the talk of a Christian justice to "people the minds of the church," a fifth implication. This phrase comes from a conversation with my friend, Bill Cotton, a distinguished, retired pastor in Des Moines, Iowa. I understand Cotton to mean by this that we need to move down the ladder of abstraction, that we need concrete words and images, and that we need to speak in the linguistic patterns and practices of flesh and blood people. Sylvia Woods, a laundry worker and labor organizer, said it well: "You have to tell people things they can see."[31] But Cotton is saying more than this. He's saying that the minds of the people of the church need to be filled with images of actual people so that when we address the powerful captivities of our time, we see people we know or people we could know who are caught in these enslaving conditions.

For example, I did not begin to think seriously about gay and lesbian people until the late sixties. At Saint Paul School of Theology several members of our faculty developed good relationships with the gay community when I first went to the school. I distinctly remember that one of the reasons I wanted to know more about and work with the gay community was that a friend of my mother's, when I was growing up, had a brother (I will call him "Roy") who was gay. My mother told me in no uncertain terms that if she ever heard of me mistreating that boy, she would "whup my ass." My mother did not have a "progressive" view of homosexuality. I doubt that she ever used the word *heterosexism*. I am quite confident that she never thought of heterosexism as a principality and power. My guess is that she was abstractly "against" homosexuality. But Roy *peopled* her mind. So when the issue came up, he was the person she thought of. It made all the difference in the world.

Basic to peopling the minds of the church is story. While I will have occasion to return to the matter of story later, a word needs to be said about the role of narrative in talking the talk. John Milbank argues that story is

---

30. Berry, "Caught in the Middle," 30–31.
31. Quoted in Howard Zinn, *A People's History of the United States*, 397.

a more basic category than understanding or explanation, that story is the way that we give an account of our lives, that we live in a story.[32]

This certainly suggests that some of the stories we live in are the stories of the principalities and powers. In the United States, for example, we tend to identify up and blame down, that is, we want to be like the rich and the celebrity; we want to be Number 1. American individualism, the Horatio Alger myth, and rags to riches narratives captivate us. We are enthralled by a movie like *Pretty Woman* where Julia Roberts plays a really good person who is a high-class prostitute who "services" a super-rich millionaire, played by Richard Gere. They, of course, fall in love and live happily ever after. Or, think of the six "Rocky" movies where the Sylvester Stallone character is able to go from the streets of Philadelphia to the heavyweight championship of the world. He is able finally to meet all the challenges out of sheer will, a rigorous training program with a good manager, and his love for his girlfriend and later his wife, Adrian. Movies like these become virtual liturgies of the American dream of successful individuals who rise up from the bottom of society to overcome any circumstance and go to the very top. We worship the dream. We identify up.

But we blame down. There are the theories of poverty that basically participate at some level in blaming the poor. The poor are poor, some argue, because they have cognitive deficiencies and lower IQs. Or they are inculcated into a culture of poverty; they are not cultivated to embody mainstream values. They suffer, for example, from a disparagement of work, a present-time orientation that does not adequately take into account the future, unstable families, early introduction of children into sexual activity, a lack of moral virtue, and so forth. Or the poor are deficient in human capital. They lack education or work skills or they need training and job experience.[33]

Interestingly, all of these theories have popular expressions by the dozens. "These poor people are just not smart." "They won't work!" "They have their minds on right now; they need to plan for the future." "All they do is sleep around." "These poor women just keep getting pregnant so that they can get more welfare." "They don't raise their children right, these kids are

32. Milbank, *Theology and Social Theory*, 267.
33. Royce, *Poverty and Power*, 63. Royce does a devastating analysis of the cognitive deficiency, the culture of poverty, and the human capital views of poverty. It is one of the best single sources for this kind of critique and offers, in addition, an alternative structural analysis with basic policy suggestions for addressing poverty. It is a lively resource for telling a much better story about the poor.

out on the street doing anything they want." "They need to learn discipline, to sober up, and to quit wasting their money."

These theories and popular expressions are based in narratives that do not hold up under close investigation. About cognitive deficiencies, studies show that only about 10 percent of the differences in wages and income can be attributed to the differences between the poor and others. Cognitive ability is hardly a major factor in poverty. Besides, I know some millionaires that are dumb as a snake. They "earned" their money the old fashioned way, they inherited it.

About the culture of poverty, while mainstream values are difficult to sustain in impoverished circumstances, the great majority of poor people already "live respectable lives," as Edward Royce reports, "working hard at thankless jobs, raising their children as best they can, tending to their communities. They do not need resocialization, government supervision, or an education in the rules of the game."[34]

Joel Schwartz, however, recommends that we fight poverty with virtue, particularly the virtues of diligence, sobriety, and thrift. But Royce wonders how far such virtues will go. He acknowledges that such virtues may benefit some who compete with undisciplined rivals in the labor market, but such virtue will not go nearly far enough given the limitations of jobs that pay a living wage. Royce questions how far lives of such virtues will go to diminish poverty in its aggregate numbers. He does notice that Schwartz fails to include virtues like militancy, solidarity of the poor with each other, and political activism, or, I would say, even public citizenship.

For the last year and a half I have been active with a fast-food workers campaign attempting to get fifteen dollars an hour and a union. Joe, a fictional name for a man I know, who has a wife and three children, works more than sixty hours a week at $7.65 an hour. A diligent, sober, and thrifty man, his employers will not permit him to work full time or more for three reasons: to avoid paying him overtime, to prevent him from becoming eligible for the Affordable Care Act, and because they prefer to hire most workers only for the rush hours of the business. His fast-food company is a national chain owned by a billionaire family, one of the richest families in the world.

The human capital theory holds that people are poor because they lack education, training, and job skills. Again, Royce demonstrates conclusively that people lack education, training, and job skills because they are poor! We hear stories about the skill deficit, but we do not hear about the job

34. Ibid.

deficit. We hear idealized stories about the job market, that it is a place where skills get you good pay and living wages, but Royce's research reveals that human ability and skill are not easily translated into jobs and high pay. Intervening factors like race, gender, culture, psychology, and social capital play powerful roles in determining the success of people. As Royce states, "Success or failure is not just due to what you know, it is also contingent on who you are, who you know, and where you work."[35]

Hence, basic to talking the talk is learning to out narrate the stories of the powers. Indeed, to name these stories as narratives of captivity. We do this by speaking in the concrete language of flesh and blood people, by telling people things they can see, by identifying and challenging the stories that blame poverty on the poor and that lead us to identify up and blame down; these are directions for talking the talk that matters.

6. *Putting the World's Story in God's Story*

The last implication for talking the talk is an attempt to counter stories that become idolatrous. I mean that activity when we place God's story in another story and make the latter the determinative narrative. These stories of the world can be about everything from the nation state to a capitalist economy to self-fulfillment. Being placed in these stories, God's story then serves these stories rather than the other way around, that is, they are idolatrous stories. Talking the talk requires the skill to place the stories of the world in God's story. This practice is basic to and underlies all of the previous implications.

My friend Jimmy Hope Smith grew up in Alabama. While no one in his family ever went to college, he was encouraged to do so by his teachers in high school. His undergraduate work and his sense of call to ministry gave his professors in college good reason to encourage him to go to seminary, which he did. He was further invited to do a PhD and wrote his dissertation on aesthetics. He has a firm grasp of that discipline in people like Kant, Hegel, Croce, Adorno, Langer, and others.

Jimmy Hope loves to go to a party and talk about art, but he does so in a thick Southern accent that he not only refuses to change but sometimes exaggerates, this being the result of an East Coast professor who told him he must lose his Southern ways of speech. From that time on he determined he would speak Southern the rest of his life. So when he goes to a party and begins to talk about art, he does so with a heavy accent tailored to get a rise

---

35. Ibid., 84.

from his conversation partners. They think he's dumb and proceed to try to make him look bad. Making Jimmy Hope look bad about art is like French kissing a rattlesnake.

Now Jimmy Hope has a father in Alabama that he genuinely loves, but his father is unredeemed in several dimensions of his life. Jimmy Hope is clear about this. When Jimmy Hope goes home to see his daddy, he reports this scene. In his daddy's house the first one up in the morning turns on the TV. The last one to bed at night turns it off. The glow of the television activates the room all day. You eat breakfast, lunch, and supper in front of it. You take naps in front of it. You entertain company in front of it. There is one sacred time, when the soap opera *As the World Turns* is on, during which no one talks, except for brief comments on individual members of the cast.

One day Jimmy Hope is visiting his daddy. They are having a wonderful conversation while watching TV. Suddenly, the face of Jesse Jackson appears on the screen. When he does, Jimmy Hope's daddy barks out, "That SOB. Somebody ought shoot him! They just ought to shoot him!"

"Daddy, do you really believe that? Do you really believe somebody ought to shoot Jesse Jackson?" asks Jimmy Hope.

"Yeah, I do, somebody just ought to shoot the SOB."

"Well, daddy, if you really believe that, I think you ought to go to church and pray for somebody to shoot Jesse Jackson."

"What's the matter with you, boy? Are you crazy?"

"Naw, daddy, I just think if you really believe that, you ought to go to church and pray for somebody to shoot Jesse Jackson."

"Boy, you know good and well that Jesus ain't gonna put up with that shit."

Notice that Jimmy Hope did not appeal to human rights or the work of civil rights organizations, and certainly not to the range of legitimate academic authorities he could easily call upon. None of those would have meant a thing to his father. What Jimmy Hope knew was that with all his foibles his father believed there were no flies on Jesus. What Jimmy Hope did was to place his father's narrative about killing Jesse Jackson into Jesus's story. This is the skill of talking the talk, the placing of the world's stories in God's story.

None of this, of course, is to neglect the importance of walking the walk in a Christian justice. We turn there next.

Chapter 4

WALKING THE WALK

In the mid-sixties three very young men—eighteen to twenty years old—decided to burn their draft cards in protest of the Vietnam War on the steps of the courthouse in South Boston, at that time a strong Irish ethnic neighborhood. These young men, all of small stature, were brutally beaten by a group of "toughs" on the scene. I saw them the next day. The eyes of one young man were swollen beyond the bone structure of his face; he peered at me through narrow slits between his eyelids.

The decision was made to protest this beating by organizing a march from that courthouse to the Boston Commons, a large park downtown. Some who joined the march supported the burning of draft cards, others did not, but all were convinced that the beating was criminal and could not be ignored.

When we showed up that day, there were some two hundred of us, a hundred police, and about six hundred antidemonstrators. It was an ominous scene. One of the organizers of the march instructed Ed Blackman and me to go to the end of the line of march. I said OK, but asked why he wanted us there. He told us we were two of the bigger people, and he wanted us there because it was the place where we were more likely to be attacked. I am not a terribly brave man, and I distinctly remember being put off by the fact that the demonstrators—at this march, at least—were so small.

About six feet tall and weighing in at about 220 pounds, Ed Blackman was a United Church of Christ urban minister. Around thirty, he had been deeply involved in the civil rights movement and was a veteran of many demonstrations. At six feet three inches, weighing in at about 190 pounds, and having just finished a PhD at Boston University, I was a novice at this kind of demonstration, especially one so menacing.

When the march began, antidemonstrators started running through the middle of the march throwing punches. They were experienced street fighters. I remember a conversation I had once with a man who had a considerable local reputation for being a formidable scrapper; he told me not ever to try to hit someone in the head in a street fight. "You too often miss; go for the gut." The antidemonstrators were running through our lines and pounding people in the stomach. I was completely stopped; I had no idea of what to do. Suddenly, Ed began to run to where the antidemonstrators were attacking our line. He started shouting to the police and pointing at individual attackers, "Officer, arrest that man. I will personally press charges!" He pointed to another attacker and yelled to another police officer, "Arrest him, I will press charges!" Running behind Ed and following his lead, I began to do the same thing. I was amazed. Within a minute the attack ceased.

Had it not been for Ed's capacity to size up the situation and to act quickly and effectively, that day would have turned far worse.[1] Ed Blackman was not just lucky there; he was not only brave; he brought to that event rich experience and a skilled background in conflict and nonviolence that came to him in a crunch. He knew what he was doing. I also do not mean to suggest that God was not with us in that violent conflict. I do mean to suggest that God's presence and power also operates in human skill and know-how, like that of Ed Blackman.

In chapter 1 we developed a distinctively Christian justice. In the next chapter we look at the issue of formation in the sensibilities and dispositions of a Christian justice. In chapter 3 we dealt with the importance of language, concepts, and categories and their crucial role in forming experience and addressed ways to respond to the dominant language of the powers and to challenge the reigning discourse.

In this chapter we take on the matter of walking the walk. Often this phrase is used to call people to an integrity of witness, that is, don't just talk the talk but walk the talk or walk the walk. While I do not for a moment mean to slight the importance of the integrity of walking the talk, the topic of this chapter is on *the skills* of walking the walk. The focus here is not an exhortation to faithfulness—as desperately crucial as faithfulness is—rather

---

1. Parenthetically, let me say also that the demonstration that day was probably not wise. I doubt that we actually changed anything. I now believe that had we worked ecumenically with the congregations in Southie and organized clergy and laity to address the violence against the three young men at the courthouse, we could've made a far more lasting impact, not to mention the fact that we antagonized that Irish community. I do not mean to suggest that confrontational demonstrations are always wrong; I certainly do not mean we should never agitate, but there is a difference—I later learned in organizing—between agitation and irritation.

the purpose of this chapter is to name and describe the material practices necessary to walking the walk of a Christian justice.

THE CRAFT TRADITION OF KNOWING

I will work here out of what philosopher Alasdair MacIntyre calls the craft tradition of knowing.[2] It is a tradition where in order to know how to work in a tradition, the knower has to be shaped by the object or the art or the practice to be known, or, better here for my purposes, the apprentice must be shaped by the work to be done. You cannot learn to be a catcher by playing tennis or vice versa, though of course there are aspects of each that can crossover, such as conditioning, eye-hand coordination, and so on. Still, you learn and are formed to do an activity by the practice and performance of that activity. You have to walk the walk to learn and be formed.

When I was young, I worked five summers in the oil field as a roust-about, basically a laborer who works not on a drilling rig but out and about in the field. I learned that my opinions as a college student did not teach me to lay a pipeline. I had to learn about big pipe, how to lift it, how to make it up (screw pipe together or weld it) and what was required of me to be able to develop the skills and know-how of working in the field. I was clearly an apprentice. Working in the oil field is a tradition, so is baseball, so is tennis.

The Christian faith is, of course, also a tradition, and justice is a tradition within the faith. I want to suggest that justice within the Christian tradition requires more than mere knowing about. As I said in the previous chapter, a Christian justice involves formation; it also requires know-how.

KNOW-HOW VERSUS KNOW ABOUT

It is one thing to know about something. I know about a lot of things that I do not know how to do. I know about skiing, but I know very little about how to ski. I know about the two-step in dance. I can even do a primitive two-step, but when I am in a fine honky tonk surrounded by

2. MacIntyre, *After Virtue*, 222. McIntyre argues against simplistic or rigid notions of tradition by stating that a tradition is a socially embodied, historical extended argument about the goods of a tradition. This is an important notion to develop against those who see tradition as a narrow, authoritarian, lock-step rigidity that cannot address change and new challenges.

extraordinary two-step dancers, it is clear that I know little about how to do that wonderful dance, which can be a display of high skill and aesthetic art!

Notice how people who are among the best in their fields of work not only know about the field but know how to perform in that endeavor. On January 20, 2014, Ellen DeGeneres had on her TV show the extraordinary actor, Meryl Streep. As DeGeneres often does, she devised a scheme to see how Streep would handle spontaneously some challenge, in this case, some "acting" assignments for which Streep had not been informed ahead of time. The first assignment was for her to sight-read a recipe in a very sexy way. Streep simply drilled it. It is hard to imagine that anyone could have done it better had one had time to prepare. The second assignment was for Streep to read directions to a place as a woman in labor. Streep nailed it, which is what she did with the third assignment, which was to read a Wikipedia selection as a rebellious and angry teenager talking to her mother. Streep handled all three of these assignments consummately, a delightful testimony to her extraordinary skill as an actor. This is know-how.

But Streep is a famous actress at the top of her profession. How about our more common life together? How about flesh and blood people who live down on the ground of everyday life, like most of us? My wife, Peggy, and I were traveling by car from Phoenix to Kansas City and stopped for an overnight at a motel in Elk City, New Mexico. The next morning we went to the cafe of the motel for breakfast. Only one waitress had showed up that morning, and she had a room of diners that filled up nine of the twelve tables in the room. We sat down at an empty table and were greeted by this energetic sixty-year-old waitress who told us that she had been waiting on tables for forty-two years and still enjoyed her work. We greeted her in return, and I ordered decaf coffee.

She said, "I put on a new pot when I saw you walk into the room." She had seen that I was old, intuited correctly that I drank decaf coffee, and anticipated my order.

Peggy ordered, and then I asked for two eggs, bacon, and a bowl of oatmeal, a sizable meal that would hold me for the six hours before we would have lunch. When the waitress brought my order, she said, "I only brought you a cup of oatmeal, because our bowls are very big. I thought you could only eat a cup. So I saved you money. If you want more, I will be glad to refill the cup."

She was exactly right. By the time I finished the meal, I had had plenty. During our time there, I began to watch her work with people at the other tables. She had something different to offer those at each table and carried on conversations that seemed specific to each of the diners and not some hackneyed, routinized chatter that she had developed of a habitual kind. Meanwhile she carried on a conversation with us that was specific to the information we offered. She would, upon returning to our table, take up that conversation again where we had left off before. Here was a waitress with know-how, a waitress who knew what she was doing and was thoroughly competent at it.

I think of the practice of a Christian justice in these terms. It involves a distinct competence, a know-how that comes through training and experience. I once was privileged to be in the room with Ernesto Cortes while he bargained with a high official in Arizona state government. Cortes is the Industrial Areas Foundation (IAF) cochair and executive director of the West/Southwest IAF regional network. He first became known in the mid-seventies as the community organizer for the Communities Organized for Public Service in San Antonio, Texas.

In this bargaining session with the state official, I was impressed with how Cortes quietly worked with the state official to give that official everything he had to have in order to work with us. Money was a sensitive issue, for example, and the official had to have control of that by law. Cortes understood and suggested a couple of things to the official that apparently reassured the official that the money issue was solved. At the same time, Cortes bargained for everything our organization needed, and we walked out of the room with all of those settled in our favor, yet not at the disadvantage of the state official. Both men seemed pleased with the process and the outcome.

While I hasten to say that not all bargaining encounters can end this satisfactorily for both sides, I nevertheless was simply amazed. I had been in no few bargaining situations myself and had taught bargaining for twenty-five years in a class on strategies of social change. But that thirty- to forty-minute meeting in the room with Cortes and the state official remains the most highly skilled instance of bargaining I ever witnessed. I am convinced that this kind of know-how can be taught and people can be trained to develop this kind of competence and skill, though perhaps with most of us not to the mastery of a Cortes. We shall return to some of these skills below. For now, let me simply register the importance of know-how in the work of justice.

THE RELATIONSHIP OF DISCOURSE TO PRACTICE

Before moving on, I do need to say a word about the relationship of discourse to practice and the difference between people in this regard.

A story floats through the baseball world of a meeting between Ted Williams and Mickey Mantle. Acknowledged as one of the great students of hitting a baseball, Williams had a .344 lifetime batting average and 521 homers, in spite of the fact that he missed three seasons while serving in the Air Force during World War II and missed parts of two seasons during the Korean conflict. Mantle, in contrast, is arguably the most physically gifted player of all time. Possessed with great speed, a strong arm, and immense power—he is said to have once hit a ball 565 feet—Mantle, however, relied on his physical assets and not on self-conscious, explicit thinking about hitting the ball, at least not very complicated thought. In their hour-long meeting Williams and Mantle talked about hitting, with the result that Mantle did not get a single hit in his next twenty-eight times at bat! I don't doubt that Mantle did think when he hit a ball, but I suspect it was more like "see the ball out of the pitcher's hand and hit the ball."

Thelma Stevens was the executive of the Women's Division in the Methodist Church, now United Methodist Women, a great lady and fervently devoted to justice and peace across her life time. Once I sat with her for an afternoon during General Conference (the world meeting of what was then The Methodist Church) and just listened to her as she spoke of the strategies being played out by the various caucuses competing on the floor and in the hallways of the conference. I was amazed at how she articulated the positions of different rival groups and key leaders, often anticipating their arguments on the floor. Even more, I was stunned at her ability to predict in each case what the decision of the General Conference would be on issue after issue. She was an extraordinary practitioner of the art of social change whose powers of articulation and anticipation rivaled that of anyone I knew in the denomination at that time.

In contrast, I know people who are not explicitly articulate about approaches to social change but can size up situations and name effective directions for change without being able to tell you how they know what they know or why things will move in the direction they suggest. They are just far more intuitive and have some kind of "tactile grasp" of a setting and its possibilities. They do use language and concepts, but these are not so much descriptive and representative—that is, stating explicitly what a given group thinks and what it will do, as they are of a nonrepresentative kind—using expressions like "they won't like that and they will bolt and walk out." The electric fact is that we need both kinds of people in walking the walk. When you find that rare individual who has both, you are observing genius. Thelma Stevens was one of those.

APPRENTICESHIP

In the craft tradition of knowing, and, I would say, especially in the craft of justice, apprenticeship is central. Too many people in the church seem convinced that just having a position on a justice issue is about all you need. I hope I can disabuse anyone of that notion who reads this book and believes such things! There are, to be sure, many informal ways to apprentice oneself in justice ministry, but working with a mentor is central. To work closely with someone—like a Sam Mann, an Ernie Cortes, a Thelma Stevens, a Mac Charles Jones—is a basic practice for walking the walk of a Christian justice.

One of the best places to find and engage in apprenticeship is working closely with a competent organizer in broad-based organizing. I will address broad-based organizing in the next chapter. For now, one story. For eight years I worked closely with Joe Rubio, lead organizer for the Valley Interfaith Project in Phoenix, Arizona. I spent ten to twenty hours a week working with Rubio and others in that effort. During that time Rubio mentored me.

One day we had gone to talk with a top state official in Arizona government. During that meeting, I had become concerned about the direction of the conversation, and with that I began to lay out my hopes and vision for our proposal. We were in the early stages of developing a job training program, and I began to talk about our plan of beginning with forty to fifty students and moving in the future to as many as several hundred, with five hundred sometime in the next ten years. I could see the official's eyes glaze over.

When we left that meeting, Rubio said, "Tex, can I give you some feedback on our meeting?" "Of course," I replied. He said, "When you are meeting with a power person, as that man is, and it is not going well, do not begin to talk about your vision. Visions are a dime a dozen. Instead, begin to talk about what you are doing in organizing. Talk to him about the people we are seeing. Tell him about the relationships we have. Relationships and organized people are power. That is a far more convincing way to move."

I needed that kind of correction and mentoring, and the best way to get it is by apprenticing in a broad-based organizing effort. I can think of dozens of times when Rubio not only taught me but trained me to work in the community. We did get that job training program started, and it is now going well, but it was not built with the kind of approach I exhibited that day with the state official. This is not to say that one never speaks of a vision, but in that context and in that situation Rubio was exactly right.

SIZING UP SITUATIONS

In this same connection a word needs to be said about the capacity to size up situations. The Greeks called it *aisthesis*. It is, of course, more than mere visual perception. It seems to involve holistic use of all the senses, at least at times. It is more like a perceptual impression, a grasp that includes feeling for and a feeling into a situation. It engages the senses but it has a kinesthetic quality as well. It also grows out of experience like that of a trade, and in the case of justice issues it relates to "having been there" before.

Sam Mann was driving north on Troost in Kansas City where it intersects with 36th Street, the ghetto some would say. It was a boiling hot day, and there in the middle of the intersection he came upon an African American man beating his wife. A white man, Mann stopped the car in the intersection and got out wanting to help without further antagonizing the situation. There was no time to call the police; a police response would be too late. Mann reacted almost spontaneously. He walked toward the couple, being careful not to convey any kind of aggressive action either by bearing or posture. Mann simply said, "Please don't do that, please stop. I'm a preacher. You love this woman. You don't want to hurt her. Please stop." Sam says that he and the man looked each other in the eyes "with great recognition." I asked Sam what that meant. "I don't know, but I think he understood that I was harmless. The man responded and said simply, 'You're right.'"

With that he and Mann walked over to the sidewalk, where Mann offered to meet with him and talk. He gave the man his card and asked him to call. Meanwhile, a group of women and men stepped in to help the beaten woman, and one person got her in a car and took her away.

In Mann's car through all of this was a parishioner, an African American woman, whom he was taking to get a wheel chair for her child. In conversation with her, she told me she was scared to death that "Rev. Mann, a white man, would jump out of the car and get himself into that situation." She said she was praying and kept saying to herself, "Oh Jesus, help us get out of here safe." Her response suggests the kind of danger Mann potentially took on by this intervention.

Where does Mann get that kind of capacity to size up a situation and to respond so appropriately? How did he know how to approach the man? He knew to say *please*. He asked him to stop but uttered no threat and was careful to avoid an intimidating presence. He told the man he was a preacher, and he reminded the man that he loved the woman he was beating. Mann then walked over to the sidewalk with him and offered to meet later. I suggest that Mann's sizing up of and intervention into this situation grew out of his long ministry in the black community and a great range of practices growing out of this work. His action here was the result of rich experience in talking the talk and walking the walk.

BAROQUE POIESIS

I smile as I use this fancy concept, but it relates to the matter of sizing up a situation and offers an important insight into walking the walk. John Milbank uses this concept to name a making, a producing, a creative act, a working through a process in which you do not know where things will end up. Milbank says it is "a making where motive, will, and plan are not prior to execution." In work of this kind direction comes as the product is shaped and developed. Where you start is not where you end up. Milbanks states, "The 'idea' of [ministry] no longer precedes the work in the clergy person's mind as a reflection of the ideas of God, but instead becomes that which is conveyed as an ending to the receiver from the peculiar constitution of the work itself."[3]

Under the leadership of the Rev. Dr. Vernon Howard of the Southern Christian Leadership Conference, five of us in Kansas City filed an initiative petition calling for a vote by the citizenry to increase the minimum wage. Our proposal would increase increments in the minimum wage over the next five years until it reached fifteen dollars an hour in 2020. Collecting the requisite number of signatures, it was scheduled to go on the ballot in the next several months. The mayor and city council under pressure from certain groups in the business community countered our proposal with an ordinance that would increase minimum wage in increments up to thirteen dollars an hour by that same year. In response to the council's ordinance the hotel and restaurant association developed its own initiative petition

---

3. Milbank, *Theology and Social Theory*, 41.

to go to the voters and rescind the city council ordinance and to keep the minimum wage at $7.65 an hour.

Intervening, the reactionary Missouri House and Senate passed a law that forbade any city in the state increasing the minimum wage higher than that of the state amount. To pass this measure the legislature mixed the minimum wage limitation with other issues unrelated to it into one bill in order to get the necessary majority in both houses. Our lawyers have challenged this legislative action and are taking it to the courts. Meanwhile, Saint Louis University has filed an *amicus curiae* brief supporting our claim that the action of the legislature is illegal. So at this writing we wait for these actions to play out.

When we first began work on increasing the minimum wage, we certainly could not have predicted this sequence of events, which is to say that we have not known where this issue will come out. We continue to find ourselves in situations where we will be responding to the movement of events over these next several months or more. Meanwhile, we monitor the situation and work at building up voter support for a higher minimum wage. What happens next, we do not know, and, while I cannot imagine an occasion in a public meeting where I would use the term *baroque poiesis*, it is, nevertheless, a process in which one is engaged continually in walking the walk.

SHOWING UP AND TURN OUT

Ninety percent of justice is showing up. Getting people to appear at important meetings and actions is central to the display of public interest and civic power. Many people seem to think that, if they have a worthy cause and a good position on issues, people will flock to their meetings and actions. Rarely. In my experience getting people to show up and maximizing turn out occur mainly through a lot of hard work, meeting with people, making phone calls, and continual follow up.

In this work social media are, of course, very important and should not be neglected. They are a part of day-to-day action in getting people to turn out. They can keep people informed, remind people of the right time and place for an event. It is a good way to share the names, telephone numbers, and addresses of participants. I find, however, that they work best when an action is "hot," when people are stirred and emotions are high. They do not, however, take the place of the kind of organizing we will address in the chapter 6.

Another important practice in getting people to show up is to do sign ups, that is, getting people to indicate their intent by putting their names on sign-up sheets. It is effective but typically only half the people who sign up show—at least that's a good estimate.

I find that many clergy develop a pattern of arriving late and leaving early, especially when it comes to justice work. This is a deadly pattern. It can convey many problems: not taking justice work seriously, overscheduled lives, coming mainly out of guilt, doing what is expected, and so forth.

It is difficult to get people to show up, especially in large numbers. It requires what I have come to call scut work.

SCUT WORK

Obviously, this kind of organizing requires attention to detail; it demands anticipation and follow-up. Lena DeCicco, a social worker in Boston with whom I worked during my time there, called much of this kind of activity "scut work." She described it as the kind of thing most people don't want to do. It's making the phone calls; it's writing notes of appreciation, it's checking to make sure people do what they say they will do; it's sending out reminders of meetings and assignments, and so on. Scut work is utterly essential to walking the walk.

It is difficult to exaggerate the importance of phone calls. Robert Caro's monumental study of President Lyndon B. Johnson describes how utterly important the telephone was to Johnson. It was constantly in use by him and played no small role in his capacity to work in the Senate and later in the presidency.[4]

I recommend that the phone be used by pastors in some pretty scutty ways in the more general work of the parish. For example, in arriving at a new church, making a telephone call to all the members of the church is an impactful way to begin one's *ministry*. A few churches may be too large, but not many. I find that a hundred calls can be made in about four hours, if you stay after it. Devoting several hours a day to this work the first week or two is a fine way to make an initial connection with congregants. Most of the calls will get the answering machine so that only a brief message by the pastor is necessary. For example, "Hello, this is the Rev. Scut Miles. I am your new pastor at St. Matthew United Methodist Church. I simply want

---

4. Caro, *The Years of Lyndon Johnson*, 588–90.

to greet you and to say, if there is anything I can do as your pastor, please do not hesitate to let me know. I hope to meet you in person in the near future." I have been amazed at the appreciation members of congregations express after these calls.

In walking the walk in the work of justice, the telephone is key in staying in touch and in order to sustain relationships with a large range of people. I find phone calls especially helpful in following up e-mails and other forms of social media. An e-mail is just not enough with most people. This is especially true with getting people to show up and to get turn out for important meetings.

THREE ISSUES

These few notes, of course, do not cover the entire range of the important characteristics of walking the walk, but do identify a number of key considerations. To conclude this chapter I want to address three issues that grow from these brief notes on talking the talk and walking the walk. These three issues are not afterthoughts but rather themes that are implicit in what has gone before, but more than that, they are important conclusions of these two chapters in themselves.

The Self or the Subject

The first of these has to do with the way the self—or as I think it more accurate to say, the subject—is understood. In the West we come out of centuries that have conditioned us to think in terms of the free autonomous self. In some of this the self is perceived as prior to society. We have political thought that asserts a state of nature prior to the establishment of government. Further, if anything, this notion of a free autonomous self is exacerbated in the consumerist world we now inhabit.

One expression of this issue is a powerful tendency in our culture to see the self as something to be discovered. In this tendency the self possesses some essence that can be brought forth by a host of introspective techniques and approaches. The search for authenticity, for example, is an attempt to ferret out, to name, and to live to the fullest this essence. We are instructed to be who we are, to find our identity, to be our real selves. The usual source of problems for this view of the self is not having enough esteem or some feeling of inferiority or perhaps just lacking that technique or insight that can overcome the barriers to one's true self-expression.

Typically these views do not look at what Paul would have called the powers. These views do not examine the captivities that hold such selves in their grip. They certainly do not name this very construction of the self as a source of captivity. Out of his own frustration with such views Michel Foucault called for a refusal of the self, that is, a turning away not only from the problems of such a self but from that very understanding of the self as such. For Foucault these constructions were major captivities sustained by the constructions of normalcy that constitute the primary forms of domination. We are held in captivity by the discourses and other practices that sustain this understanding of the self.

In contrast to this essential self, I offer the concept of subject. Not some self preceding socialization but a subject constituted in the language and material practices of a form of life. There is no essence to be realized but an embodied, social creature formed and to be formed. In a view of this kind it is not necessary to reject self-reflection, but the focus is not so much on insight as on engaging the practices of formation, by which subjects in a form of life can shape their bodies, sensibilities, dispositions, skills, and makeup. I am not as interested in self-reflexivity as such as I am in the concrete practices in which it is embedded. The popular assessment of "navel gazing" is not excessive in describing those who are so focused inwardly that attention to the practices that constitute one's life take second place, sometimes distantly so.

In the church as a form of life, especially as new creation, the far more important categories are those of call and the gifts and graces we bring to the mission and work of the church. Reflection then takes place around the determination of these critical matters. Further, call and gifts and graces are languaged, perceived, trained, and performed in the community of faith. This work of communal discernment is one that develops the capacities to resist and challenge the powers and their operation in forming us as subjects. We are introduced in baptism and embodied in the righteousness of God in worship, prayer, Eucharist, life together, and in the training of the practices of liberation, mercy, and reconciliation. It is here we are formed, where we learn to talk the talk and walk the walk.

Freedom: Talk-Ability and Walk-Ability

The second issue is that of freedom. I have already challenged the consumerist notion of freedom as mere choice. At this point I need to be more descriptive of the notion of freedom as capaciousness. Understood this way freedom is not merely some freedom to make a decision, although such thoughts of freedom as merely free will require more analysis of such perceived capacities to choose. Growing up in Mississippi, I often heard the expression, "I am free, white, and twenty-one." I came to have serious questions about such expressions of supposed freedom with their explicit racist make up. I don't think people who claimed this kind of freedom typically had any idea how incarcerating such ideas were for themselves.

I am also convinced that pop expressions of freedom have problems in their obeisance to the powers: "Nobody's going to tell me what to do." "I can do what I please." "As long as I don't hurt anyone else, I am free to do what I want." It is not only the individualism in such comments that trouble me; it is the typical sense that one is able to be free in these terms. These kinds of comments hide the fact that freedom is an achievement, that it is populated with skills, that it requires discipline, that it is a profoundly social virtue.

So freedom here is understood as the capacity to move in a form of life. It involves someone so shaped in the sensibilities and dispositions of a specific time and place as to be able to talk the talk and walk the walk of that social world. Freedom comes in this kind of context as an embodied capacity with the ability to perform in that way of life. Freedom involves a kind of savoir faire, though I do not mean to suggest by this some necessarily more literate, highly educated or so-called "cultural style." When I worked in the oil field I knew men who were consummate in their ways of conduct, language, and practices, not just fitting for the job we were doing but powerfully able to draw on the motivated cooperation of others in the gang. *That* was freedom!

So in terms of a Christian justice I understand freedom as this kind of embodied talk-ability and walk-ability that grows from the training and the developed skills of an apprenticeship in the practices of a faith community, understood as new creation, where liberation, mercy, and reconciliation take on an intrinsic character in this people of the way. In this understanding of freedom as capaciousness, we acquire agency as we learn to think, talk, and move with agility and skill in the work of justice. It is knowing what can be said and done in a given setting. It suggests a know-how well acquainted with the feel and the rhythms of a situation and able to sense and move at those moments when the timing is right. This freedom can sense the ethos of a setting, can read the emotions at play, and is at work in and with the sensibilities and dispositions of a given time and place.

Sailing in the Grace of God

I hope that the passages above will not be read as works righteousness. I do not understand them in that way. It is true that I am suspicious of views that see grace as some subjective state we receive by merely trusting God. I am not impressed with certain psychological dynamics where we gain our worth simply by accepting God's grace. I don't trust it. I want to know the practices embedded in our response to God's grace. It sounds bourgeois to me, when God's grace and our response are mainly some kind of transfer inside our heads or our bourgeois hearts. The reduction of God's grace and our response as some kind of intrapsychic dynamic seems to reduce grace to the conceits of the free autonomous individual.

I do not want to be misunderstood here. Trust in God is central in Christian faith, but the self is profoundly corporate, participates in Christ, and seeks formation in his image. This is not the consumerized self, seeking out satisfaction of one's preferences in some self-realization that seems to serve no larger good, for example, that self-promoted by a thousand advertisements. Trust in God is immersion in the rich gifts and resources of God's love. It is an embodied trust, one where we do not merely entertain some proposition about God's love but where the trust involves a way of life, a talking and a walking.

I appreciate Bishop Ken Carder's take on this. Critical of those who understand grace as some "prepackaged gift dispensed by God," he insists on understanding grace as "God's presence and power." It is God's action "to create, heal, forgive, reconcile, and transform persons, communities, nations, and the entire cosmos. Where God is present there is grace, God's power to renew and transform."[5] Yes, God's grace as God's presence and power, not merely some psychic kick resulting from God's positive regard but rather a God who is present and whose power can goose us. This is the God whose "prevenient grace," in the language of John Wesley, comes to us before we ever know it.

Language of the heart is biblical language, and I heed that, but in the individualism of our culture and the subjective and peripheral language in which "religion" is cast, we must be careful in how we use these words about our internal lives in the contemporary context. For this reason, among others, I search for different metaphors for God's grace. One of these—the source of which I cannot find—is the suggestion that God's grace is like a great wind across the sea. In response to God's initiative we are called to raise a sail into that wind. This is the best metaphor for how I understand these practices of justice and the formation of our lives by the power and presence of God. God is the source and initiator of these practices, the God

---

5. Carder, *Living Our Beliefs*, 76.

who has called us into the new creation of the church. In response, we raise the sail of the practices of justice into the wind of God's grace.

SUM AND CONCLUSION

Let's review what I have said so far. While supporting a justice of human rights, I have argued for a specifically Christian justice based in the righteous act of God in Jesus Christ, a justice of liberation/deliverance, mercy, and reconciliation found in the writings of the Apostle Paul. Commitment to and engagement in this kind of justice requires formation in the sensibilities and dispositions necessary both to be and to do this kind of community of faith in witness before the principalities and powers that rule the world between the times.

Further, I have emphasized the importance of talking the talk of a Christian justice, emphasizing the importance of language as the stuff of life and the role of words, concepts, and vocabularies in shaping our experience. Given this central role of language, the skills of fluency take on major importance and open up opportunities for faithful work in talking the talk.

All of this, however, is not to diminish the key place of walking the walk, and I have made central an approach to Christian justice as a craft, emphasizing the importance not only of *knowing about* but of *know-how* in the work of social witness. Additionally, I have suggested key skills and practices to be learned in apprenticeship from able practitioners in the work of a Christian justice.

Finally, I intend that nothing I have written should be construed as a works righteousness. The righteous act of God in Jesus Christ is the towering work of grace in human history. The formation of ourselves, the development of the practices and skills of talking the talk and walking the walk are responses to what God has done in Christ in the empowering work of God's grace. To embody this, to live out a Christian justice, is to raise a sail into the wind of that righteous rule of grace that sweeps across the world.

Having said these things, we are ready to take on two key issues in the work of justice, interests and power. How are we to understand and work with these matters that ever loom before any attempt to do justice? We turn here in the next chapter.

Chapter 5

INTERESTS AND POWER

We were working with a church in a large city that may very well have more millionaires per square foot than any other church in the country. Located in a highly affluent suburb, this congregation is hardly the kind of place where you expect broad-based organizing to occur, especially with an organizing effort that works centrally with the poor, the marginal, and the oppressed. But about a half dozen members and a woman associate pastor of the congregation decided to do significant listening sessions with congregational members to discover the issues that were important to them. From this initial endeavor developed large participation in broad-based organizing.

Basic to this process, as we shall see in the next chapter, was storytelling, where participants shared stories out of their own experience relative to the issues of concern to them. In these discussions and sharing of stories they found a serious passion for public education in the church membership. With this discovered interest clearly before them, they began to seek out informed educators and experts in education and public policy so as to enrich their knowledge and build relationships in the field. They also held informative meetings where divergent points of view were presented in which a civil approach was emphasized, all to good effect.

Later, they were able to move into the issue of immigration. They did so by setting up a meeting of a dozen people with equal representation of very conservative and very liberal participants. Interestingly, these participants began to move toward one another in their points of view, taking a more moderate point of view but believing that serious immigration reform was required.

Here's the point. People of quite diverse points of view with quite different interests were able to work together, and that church became a major player in the broad-based organizing work in that city, a vital role the church continues to play.

INTERESTS

I begin with this story as a way to approach two significant matters in the work of a Christian justice for the common good, specifically interest and power. I begin first with the matter of interests and will turn to power in the second half of this chapter. First, interests, which we will discover are used in complicated ways. Let me begin with just five ways interests are often understood.

- Interests as selfishness
- Interests as rational calculation of advantage
- Interests as determined by cost benefit analysis
- Long-term interests
- Enlightened self-interests

What is interesting here is that none of these is the same. Selfishness, for example, is typically not very rational, though it can be. And rational calculation of advantage, simply named as such, does not indicate which form of rationality is at play. If we have learned anything in the last fifty years of philosophical thought, it is that rationality is not one thing but operates in any number of forms; there is no universal rationality. So the use of rational calculation strictly speaking does not tell us much. Further, interests as determined by cost-benefit analysis certainly cannot be reduced simply to rational calculation of advantage. For example, seeking advantage over a rival can be destructive of a cost-benefit action. Finally, long-term and enlightened self-interests complicate all of the above and surely cannot be reduced to anyone of the first three understandings of interests as such.

What is also quite clear is that the motivations of the affluent church members with whom I began this chapter cannot be understood in terms of any one notion of interest. Yes, I can identify some actions or moves that were selfish; and there were occasions of rational calculations of advantage and cost-benefit analysis, but when you "get into the weeds" of the conversations, storytelling, pursuit of experts in the field, the educational events they held, and the conclusions they reached, a far greater array of motivation is engaged than the five understandings of interest I have named.

The complicated uses of the word *interest* is supported by Albert Hirschman's careful study of the history of the concept in the West for roughly the last five hundred years.[1] Without going into the details of his study, it is sufficient here to say that historically, the word varies a great deal in its use across that period of time. It has no single use; it cannot be *essentially* defined, certainly not in the wide variety of ways it has been used historically. In a second book, a continuation of his research on interests, Hirschman reports the claims of a James Mill who argues that interests are necessarily rational and that therefore the concept requires a distinction between real interests and false interests. But in politics this gap between real interests and a misperception of interests can be quite broad and vexed, so much so that one Thomas B. McCaulay, in a devastating critique, seizes upon Mills's argument and dismisses it as empty. Indeed it is a tautology, McCaulay declares, if interest means that people "had rather do what" they "had rather do."[2]

Further, the notion that interests are rational requires close consideration. Daniel Kahneman, the 2002 Nobel Award–winning psychologist for his work in economics, raises sharp questions about the rationality of interests. In a chapter on "the engine of capitalism" he finds that "optimistic individuals play a disproportionate role in shaping our lives" and can play a positive role. They are often talented and "lucky." Their optimism can have a positive effect on people who work with them. Their successes can provide them with confidence about their abilities, and this assessment is usually supported by the admiration of others.[3]

This "optimism bias," however, is not an unmitigated good, argues Kahneman. He writes of "entrepreneurial delusions," where business people simply regard themselves and their decisions more highly than they should. He also offers a "hubris hypothesis" for those executives who run huge risks in taking over other companies in acquisitions and mergers. These "efforts to integrate large firms fail more often than they succeed," a result explained by the finding that "the executives of the acquiring firm are simply less competent than they think they are."[4]

Further, Kahneman reports that business leaders are often too "overconfident." One study found, for example, "that financial leaders of large corporations had no clue about the short-term future of the stock market; the correlation between their estimates and the true value was slightly less than zero!" Still, notes Kahneman, optimism is highly regarded both "socially and in the market: people and firms reward the providers of

---

1. Hirschman, *The Passions and the Interests*.
2. Hirschman, *Rival Views of Market Society*, 48.
3. Kahneman, *Thinking, Fast and Slow*, 255–65.
4. Ibid., 257ff.

dangerously misleading information more than they reward truth tellers." One other failing: business leaders often ignore what the competition is doing when they make marketing decisions: "the competition is simply not part of the decision."[5]

Kahneman is clear that "the effects of high optimism on decision making are a mixed blessing, but the contribution of optimism to good implementation is certainly positive."[6] The main reason for this is the resilience it offers in the face of frustrating circumstances where people nevertheless persist and some become successful. Perhaps because of the contribution optimism makes, Kahneman offers from his colleague Gary Klein "a partial remedy" called "the pre-mortem." This practice is used when a corporation has almost come to a key decision, but just short of implementation. At that point the board of the corporation is asked to imagine the complete failure of this decision about a year hence. Each person present is then asked to take five to ten minutes to compose a short chronicle of what went wrong.[7]

What I love about Kahneman's research is that when one "gets into the weeds" of corporate pursuits of their "interests," hard-nosed interests of rational calculation and cost-benefit analysis take on considerably less credibility. But my basic point here is that the word *interest* is, on the one hand, a highly variable concept. Its meaning is determined by its use. It has no essence that can be applied like a template on the motivations or actions of people. On the other hand, the notion that interests can be simply understood as a rational process attending to advantage or some cost-benefit analysis of a situation is quite simply a gross simplification and distortion of human motivation and decision making.

INTERESTS: STORY AND TRADITION

Yet, in broad-based organizing, which we consider in the next chapter, interest is a key concept and one constantly in use. It needs to be said, however, that it is not simplistically understood. In his study of broad-based organizing Jeffrey Stout finds that organizers often work with the concept of interest "in the narrow sense," that is, self-interest. Stout explains that most people will not initially have a more expansive view, that is, "living in a community freed from domination." One of the things that organizing does, maintains Stout, is to open up people to the common good, and by

5. Ibid., 261–64.
6. Ibid., 263.
7. Ibid., 264–65.

doing so this enables them to see how typical notions of self-interest and the way they function prevent the kinds of relationships that people actually do need to endorse and enjoy.[8] Stout takes note of the fact that organizers do urge people to be honest about their interest in this narrow sense, and he indicates that a lot of hard work is required to expand the meaning of interest and to demonstrate how interests "can converge in the common good of the community as a whole." He further comments that "the grass roots democratic organizer... resists the reduction of politics to the negotiation of preferences and the coordination of interest groups in the narrow sense of 'interest.'"[9] I might add here that the experience of the congregation in that highly affluent suburb, with which we began this chapter, illustrates this kind of transformation of interests quite graphically.

So, I appreciate Stout's point here and agree with it. I do, however, want to expand on the notion of interest and place it in an explicit relationship with story, tradition, and loves. I remember when Joe Rubio once told me, "We don't know what are our interests are until we have a story." Rubio saw a direct connection between story, the intensity of an interest, and its context. On Rubio's view, these provide the energy so necessary to organizing.

We were doing organizing around the housing crisis in Arizona in 2008–2010. I remember specifically a visit we made to the mayor of a Phoenix suburb in which we were going to ask him to work with us in that effort. In the premeeting of our organizing team, someone informed us that this mayor held to a virtually fundamentalist, neoclassical, free market, capitalist ideology. He would not take kindly to any suggestion that the market had failed. We needed his cooperation, but an approach critical of the market would get us a long rant, a very brief conversation, and no cooperation. We decided that in the meeting after introductions we would simply begin with this story: a Hispanic couple, legal residents of the United States, but still not highly proficient in the use of English, understood that they bought a house from an agent. Making a down payment of thirty thousand dollars, they then made the stated contractual payments promptly for the next twelve months. At the end of that year they received a letter from the agent indicating that they had thirty days to move out of the house. When they protested that they were the owners of the house, they were told they were only leasing the house, as in fact it read in the fine print of the document they signed. They had paid thirty thousand dollars down just to lease the

8. Stout, *Blessed Are the Organized*, 41.
9. Ibid., 217.

house. Upon hearing this story, the mayor became incensed and agreed not only to work with us but to be present and to make a supportive comment at our coming action.

There is no question that this mayor typically understood interest in terms of the logics of a free market economy. His view of a human being would be that of some kind of cost-benefit choice maker competing for economic advantage in a free market. But the story of this disciplined but victimized couple led him in the direction of the common good. Such is the "alchemy" of the way that interest is used in the work of broad-based organizing.

The story, taken alone, however, is not enough. I contend that all of us operate out of traditions, usually more than one. Even those who decry tradition operate out of some tradition, even if implicitly and not knowingly. Stories occur in, operate out of, are interpreted by, embody, and perform traditions. Further, interests are relative to traditions. We do not understand interests apart from stories and the traditions in which they move and function, and, indeed, which they instantiate. While we were careful not to attack the mayor's free enterprise tradition, we failed to recognize before that meeting that his tradition of free enterprise did operate, as it turned out, with a powerful narrative of fair play. It was this narrative within his free enterprise tradition that was central and brought forth his enraged response to the injustice perpetrated against the Hispanic couple.

It is important to say also that traditions open up spaces of interest variously understood. The positive protocols that enable traditions to pursue the goods distinctive to them at the same time offer angles of advantage and opportunities to skirt around the prohibitions and constraints of the rules. Once again, look at baseball as a tradition. In that tradition a pitcher is within the rules when he or she grips a ball variously by the seams or across the seams to throw the ball to a hitter. A pitcher can pursue his and his team's advantage by using these licit pitches. The ball can also be held legitimately in different ways to throw a slider, a curve, or a knuckle ball. Yet all of these legitimate ways to pitch a ball and to seek advantage appropriately "open up spaces" by which a pitcher can be tempted to throw illegal pitches. If you know enough to throw a ball, say a curve, you also know that getting saliva or some sticky substance on a ball illegally can make the ball break even more and thus be even harder to hit. The point is that licit and illicit advantages are opened up by the very structuring that occurs in a tradition. But this is only one form interest can take. A ballplayer can also play the game in ways that serve him but may not help the team win. The player intent on looking good may not be willing to give himself up for the team, say, by refusing to bunt a ball to advance a teammate on the bases, but instead tries to hit the ball out of the park when the percentages are against the likelihood of that happening. Or, I think of the ballplayer who feigns sickness because his team is facing a pitcher on the opposing team who is extremely effective.

So it is in organizing. Knowing the tradition or traditions out of which various actors, institutions, and agencies operate, knowing the compelling stories of these same people and groups, are essential to grasping the political realities engaged in the work of organizing and in political efforts for justice. Traditions also open up illicit advantages, and these can be pursued to the detriment of the common good. We hear stories of politicians on the take or corporations that seek unlawful profit or attempt illegally to control the market. In our approach to the suburban mayor, we were, quite candidly, fortunate to tell the story we did. I don't think any of us realized how powerfully it would affect the mayor. But that it did is compelling testimony to the role of stories and traditions in structuring interests, and yes, also in opening up opportunities for engaging effectively someone like the mayor.

INTERESTS AS LOVES

Finally, I want to take the concept of interest one more step and to suggest that it be examined in terms of Augustine's *The City of God*. In his classic statement he distinguishes the two cities that "were created by two kinds of love: the earthly city created by self-love reaching the point of contempt for God, the Heavenly City by the love of God carried as far as contempt of self." The earthly city seeks glory for itself and from others. It is ruled by the "lust for domination." The earthly city lords itself over the princes and nations it subjugates. Living by human standards, it pursues the goods of the body and the mind. Even those able to know God do not honor or give thanks to God but sink into futility in their thinking with darkened and senseless hearts. Under the domination of pride they exalt themselves in their wisdom and worship idols.

In polar contrast, the heavenly city exalts and finds its highest glory in God. By God alone is the heavenly city lifted up. People are ruled in love, "the rulers by their counsel, the subjects by obedience." The heavenly city loves and seeks its strength from God alone. It seeks the wisdom that can come only from devotion to and the right worship of the true God. For its reward it turns to "the fellowship of the saints, not only holy men but also holy angels, 'so that God may be all in all'" (1 Cor 15:28).[10]

In referencing Augustine, I do not wish to pursue further his characterization of the two cities as such, but rather to examine interests in terms of what people love.[11] In my work in organizing, the most rewarding conversations I have in terms of understanding someone and getting at the heart of their energy and commitments occur when I discover what they love. This may seem to contradict what I have said above in terms of story and tradition, but I do not find it to be so. Rather, I find that the deepest layer of interest—meaning by that the level of commitment, the passion that fuels it, the extent of its embodiment, and the performative commonplace of it—resides in the loves of the person or group. To say this is not to leave story and tradition but to see love functioning in them. Our key stories and traditions are—to use a phrase out of Alasdair MacIntyre, but differently— "socially embodied and historically extended" loves.[12] These stories and traditions are not usually of one kind but can be profoundly conflicted and contradictory. Hence the reason why interests can so often fly in the face of other commitments. For example, "the lust for domination," which Augustine scores, is carried by a host of stories and resides in many traditions. Even more, it cannot be simplistically conceived.

I was once part of a church group that attempted to do conflict resolution with a congregation that had literally gotten into a fist fight with a small group of Black Panthers at the end of a worship service. It took hours to get the church to withdraw charges and to schedule conversations to work through at least some of the issues. We then went to the prosecuting attorney of the city to inform him of the church's decision and to get his office to cooperate with this approach. In effect, we asked him to withdraw the charges by the city and to allow us to work it through between the two parties. We stated that this was more consistent with the way the church dealt with such things.

Initially, he offered the position of a law enforcement agent that he could not let the Panthers off the charges, because it would condone this

---

10. Augustine, *The City of God*, bk. XIV, chap. xxviii.

11. I am indebted to Stanley Hauerwas, who suggested in a telephone conversation several years ago that I look at the issue of interest in terms of the loves in Augustine's two cities. He, of course, is not responsible for what I do here with Augustine.

12. This comes from McIntyre's *After Virtue*, 222, where he says, "A living tradition is an historically extended, socially embodied argument, and an argument precisely in part about the goods which constitute that tradition."

kind of illegal behavior. We indicated that we thought the church, the Panthers, and the community would be better served if we were allowed to work on the matter and to settle it by building better relations between the congregation and the Panthers. We noticed that he was quite resistant to this idea, but we kept pushing for our solution until he finally said, "Look, if you think I am going to forego the kind of political advantage I will lose if I do not press this action against the Panthers, you just don't get it."

There were at least two stories and traditions operating in the prosecuting attorney. One was that of law enforcement; the other was that of a political career. It was the latter that was "the deeper love." We were not successful in changing his mind; we were able to get the penalties reduced and to avoid the incarceration of the young Panthers, but only after the prosecuting attorney played out what was apparently his basic interest, really, his true love.

Yet, the play of stories, traditions, interests, and loves does not necessarily take a negative character. Very positive avenues for justice can occur when people tell their stories and speak explicitly out of the traditions that form them and which they inhabit. Furthermore, stories do bond people. They generate relationships where before none existed. Yet, they do more than bond. Stories call forth aspects or dimensions, or wisdom from traditions not previously at play in the process. The richness of traditions can offer major contributions to the common good, and open the door for traditions to offer resources not even under consideration until the sharing of stories begins. Sometimes, too, stories can modify a tradition, as that tradition rises to take on new challenges. In all of these, interests/loves operate through stories and traditions. In describing the role of self-interests, Ernesto Cortes says it this way: "The potential of ordinary people fully emerges only when they are able to translate their self-interests in issues such as family, property, and education into the common good through an intermediary organization."[13]

POWER

A second major issue in the quest for the common good is the issue of power. How to understand power and its use are utterly critical. On this matter Bernard Loomer's article on two conceptions of power has become a classic in broad-based organizing. Defining power first as "the ability to

---

13. Cortes, "Reweaving the Social Fabric," 6–7, http://new.bostonreview.net /BR19.3/cortes.html.

produce an effect," and thereby "indicating a capacity to level a shaping and determining influence on the other" are basic to power. Such a view, however, is important not only in terms of making the possible actual but also in the range of individual and social fulfillment that can be attained by the use of power. Even so, matters like these, says Loomer, raise the issue of quality of life, maintaining that the power to influence, to survive, or to dominate others does not adequately address the issues of life's most important concerns.[14]

Loomer thus distinguishes unilateral and relational power. The former makes the value of a person dependent on the influence one can exert, which obscures and neglects other values required for full living. Also, the unilateral view of power is a zero-sum game: for one group to have power, the other must experience loss of power. On this understanding, one group's power depends on the reduction of the other group's freedom. Further, with the inequalities that are inevitably part of personal and group life, the resulting inequalities related to power extend and deepen the estrangements of the losers in this power game. But the winners also lose because of the constrictive character of life lived in behalf of linear power, taken alone. Indeed, Loomer claims, life lived in pursuit of linear power enacts revenge on its actors: in the narrowing of life, in the repression of other vital energies beyond those of power as such, in the denial of communal life, in the loss of the deeper mystery of existence, and in the lack of sensibility for the other. This constriction of life—the captivity to power in its too exclusive usage and purpose, and the deadening of human sensibilities—"blocks the full flow of energy" that makes for a greater range of capacities and human completion.[15]

Relational power, on the other hand, is understood both as "the ability to produce and to undergo an effect."[16] This receiving of influence and impact, however, is not just some passive receptivity, it is rather "an active openness."[17] Were we absolutely unable to receive any kind of influence, we could not be a self at all, because each of us is constituted of our relationships. The individual emerges from profoundly "mutual relationships," making the self communal in its very makeup; it "does not have experiences, it *is* its experiences." Further, on Loomer's view, it is these constituting relations of the self that make freedom possible.[18]

---

14. Loomer, "Two Conceptions of Power," 5–32.
15. Ibid., 9–15.
16. Ibid., 17.
17. Ibid., 19.
18. Ibid.

In his description here of relational power, I think of the compelling story from the motion picture *The Miracle Worker*. Helen Keller, blind and deaf and unable to communicate with words, and her teacher, Ann Hathaway, are out in the yard of her house at the water pump. Keller is splashing the water from the pump with one hand while Hathaway writes the letters of the word *water* on the palm of the other. Keller grows frustrated and angry and resists Hathaway, fighting her, but Hathaway keeps on and on. Then there is that moment when Keller gets it, when the relationship of language and letter signs and water becomes clear. That clairvoyant moment when Keller begins the long walk in the use of language and the freedom that bursts forth in her future by her having received the capacity to communicate via words.[19] Extend this story as metaphor to the range of linguistic and other practices that forms us and gives us the capacity to act and to be acted upon. This is the life giving, the freedom, and the capaciousness of relational power.

So it is in working for the common good. Relational power is that expression of give and take that grows from practices of life together and mutual conversation. Loomer speaks expressly to the importance of "being present to one another," that is, not only to reveal oneself to the other but also to assist the other in doing the same. This kind of meeting of each other recognizes the inequalities that characterizes every one. The gifts and graces of people range widely. The challenge on Loomer's view is to open up the opportunities and to enrich the relationships so that members of a group are "transformed into individuals and groups of greater stature."[20] This means not only that individual members complement each other. It also means that individuals can be trained and transformed to take on new capacities. This is why personal and group development are so important in working for justice. To watch the growth of people and the development of their skills in this work is a gift of relational power.

I taught Sunday school at our church in Phoenix. In that class was a young lawyer, Jessica Johnson, who worked with a federal agency. In her first year as a member of the class, she hardly said a word. She was painfully shy. I remember thinking how unusual it was for a lawyer not to say anything. When our church became active in the Valley Interfaith Project (VIP), the IAF organizing affiliate in Phoenix, she accepted an invitation to be a representative of our church.

---

19. *The Miracle Worker*, directed by Arthur Penn, screenplay by William Gibson, starring Anne Bancroft and Patty Duke, 1962.
20. Loomer, "Two Conceptions of Power," 26.

Possessing a sharp mind, and once trained in organizing and given the opportunity to work with groups and to develop relational skills, she became a strong leader. After being in VIP for a couple of years, she was asked to preside at a large event—about 250 people—where we had invited the Democratic and Republican candidates for mayor to respond to questions in which we asked them to support our organization's agenda. In the invitation sent to the candidates it was explicitly stated that this was not to be a time of electioneering but rather one for a direct response to our questions.

First up at the meeting was the Republican candidate. He was not more than a couple of minutes into his remarks when he left our prepared questions and launched into his campaign speech. Johnson stopped him cold, reminding him of his agreement not to electioneer and to answer the questions we had asked. He did. When the Democratic candidate for mayor went to the speaker's stand, he, too, rather quickly went into his campaign speech and moved away from our questions. The chair promptly stopped him, reminded him of the agenda, and instructed him to address our questions. He did.

With the media in attendance, our chair made several TV news shows that evening and the biggest newspaper in town the next day, specifically for the way she handled both candidates. This is exactly the kind of development that happens when people engage in broad-based organizing. It is the formation of this kind of stature—to use Loomer's term—in people that grows from training in relational power. This kind of growth in leadership capacity, moreover, redounds back into the local congregation as well, not to mention the kind of training that occurs for people to be active citizens in the larger community. These are exercises in working for the common good.

POWER: DISCOURSE AND VISIBLE PRACTICES

Still, I want to look further into the matter of power, especially in terms of the practices of power. I am instructed by Michel Foucault, a twentieth-century French philosopher, for whom power is central to his thought. I find him especially valuable for his emphasis on practices in his approach to power, practices related both to the languaging of power (discourse) and other more visible practices (nondiscursive). For Foucault power is the effect of a network of practices, a definition that can certainly include Loomer's distinction between unilateral and relational power, but his focus on the practices of power makes it more concrete.[21] On Foucault's view power "is not an institution, a structure, or a certain force with which people are endowed." It is rather "a complex strategic relation" within societies and between individuals. That is, power cannot be possessed by an individual, an institution, and so forth, but rather it exists in and as relationship. As Foucault says, "It is exercised rather than possessed." In this sense power flows and circulates through people and their organized lives. Anthropologist Talal Asad, influenced by Foucault, describes power as "the effect of an entire network of practices."[22]

With his focus on practices Foucault provides what he calls "an ascending analysis of power." That is, he examines the micro practices of power, the "infinitesimal mechanisms of power" or, as I like to call them, the granular practices of power. Foucault also states that his approach is "to locate power at the extreme points of its exercise."[23] All of this suggests that we look at power down on the ground of its exercise at the bottom of a community.

As part of the organizing work in Phoenix, we discovered that Hispanic families were having trouble with a criminal element that would move into and control their neighborhood, because the people in those neighbors were afraid to call the police. While the great majority of these families were citizens or legally in the United States, nevertheless some had family or neighbors who were not legally documented. Hence they did not call the police out of fear that these legally vulnerable people would be arrested and deported. A criminal element knew how to take advantage of this kind of situation and would come in and dominate the neighborhood.

Our organizing effort invited the chief of police to do neighborhood walks with us to meet these families. Having met with the chief on several occasions, we knew his position. He had stated clearly that he and his police department had all they could do just to combat violent crime in Phoenix. He also did not see his department as an arm of the immigration office of the federal government. In effect he said to the families that his officers were not there to enforce immigration law but to serve the people there and prevent the kind of criminal takeovers of neighborhoods that were occurring.

One night in a neighborhood the chief had visited, a man was beating his wife. One of the women the chief had talked with when he walked

21. For my fuller treatment of Foucault's view of power see my recent book, *Human Nature, Interest, and Power: A Critique of Reinhold Niebuhr's Social Thought*, esp. 76–84.

22. Asad, *Genealogies of Religion*, 35.

23. Michelle Foucault, *Power/Knowledge*, 99.

the neighborhood felt free to call the police to stop the beating. When the police came, they arrested her husband. In all the excitement neither he nor she had the command of English to clarify that it was the man next door and not her husband who was the offender. The police took her husband to the police car. She, however, still had the chief's card in the apartment; she grabbed it, ran out to the officers, and pointing to the card said repeatedly to them, in broken English, "Call him!" When they did, the chief said, "She's one of ours; get a translator out there to find out what's going on." They did and made the appropriate arrest.

To pursue justice is to change and introduce new practices into the relations, the flows, and the trajectories of down-on-the-ground power. When these changes occur it affects the practices of power across a host of connections and organizational levels in community. Even more, when there is a broad base of organized institutions working together for the common good, this introduces a different range of practices across a community and subsequently alters the power practices of that community.

TRUTH AND POWER

One other aspect of Foucault's view of power is important here and that is the relationship he sees between truth and power. For Foucault truth is a thing of this world, which means he does not see truth as some correspondence between a statement or a discourse and what is the ultimate state of affairs in the world.[24] Rather on his view truth amounts to a certain intelligibility between discourse and a form of life in a specific time and place. Intelligibilities change, and Foucault traces different forms of intelligibility across certain histories and in specific places, for example, in areas like discipline and punishment in dealing with criminality, in sexuality, and in asylums.

Foucault argues that power requires establishment, consolidation, and implementation through "the production, accumulation, circulation and functioning of a discourse." That is, power and truth in his sense are constituted together and are interdependent. As he says, power "is organized in a highly specific fashion" in each particular society and that "we are forced to produce the truth of power our particular society demands," to wit, the kind of power our society necessitates in order to function. Another way to say this is that truth is the way to formulate what can be said and done in a form of life.

---

24. Foucault, *Power/Knowledge*, 93.

One way to look at this is to see how important a compelling discourse is in dealing with power. We were lobbying the legislature in Arizona about state budget proposals, especially one dealing with proposed cuts on those in poverty. Four of us were talking with a state senator urging him to vote against the efforts to cut funding for the poor. He said, "Well, you know, that's the responsibility of the church. You know what Jesus said, the Bible says, 'As you have done it unto the least of these....'" His point, of course, was that this text was addressed to the church to serve those in need and that such service was the responsibility of the church, not the responsibility of the state. He smirked seeming to think that he had won the day, argument over. One of the members of our group, however, said, "How long has it been since you had a chance to look at that text? You know, it is not addressed to the church. It is addressed to the nations. The text, Matthew 25 says, that 'All the nations will be gathered before...the Son of Man,' and they will be judged on how they deal with the hungry, the thirsty, the stranger, the naked, the sick, and the imprisoned."

It simply stopped the state senator cold. He blushed, cleared his throat, and after an embarrassing pause indicated he had to go to a meeting. Yes, this is only an incident, but one that clearly indicates how important a compelling discourse is in dealing with power. Being able to "stay in the room," meaning by that being able to stand up to power with claims that are more lucid, that provide a more credible and gripping account, these are crucial in seeking the common good.

This relationship between the practices of "truth" and power is one reason why the chapters on talking the talk and walking the walk in this book are so important. So let me be clear, I believe that the revelation of God in Christ is true in the ultimate sense of the word *truth*. Yet, we never get that revelation fully right in our language, our discourse, our understanding. That is, the intelligibility with which we understand the Christian faith is not fully adequate, which is why we ever need correction and formation in faith. And, as I tried to say in the discussion on living in a world with others, why it is necessary to learn from and to be questioned by those of other traditions as well as our own. These are crucial in building the church as an alternative community, as Paul's new creation.

Meanwhile, we must not forget that we live in a world where the powers are still in control. At this point we are again helped by Foucault who introduces the concept of "regimes of truth," that is, the ruling forms of truth constituted in the established discourses and practices of a form of life. These regimes of truth manifest themselves in a host of expressions. I think of a relentless militarism and devotion to war, of idolatrous patriotism and idols of the market place, of oppressive racism, classism, sexism, and heterosexism, and of the practices of ecological devastation, to name only some. In examining issues of this moment, it is important to know that, for Foucault, these forms of power rule not so much by coercion but rather in the way that people are constituted by power, so that we are not so much coerced as socialized into them. As he says, the primary form of domination is normalization.[25]

POWER AND FORMATION FOR JUSTICE

At the same time, Foucault is clear that power is the source of our capacity to be agents and not only subjects of power. On his view power is both external and internal. If the former shapes us from without, the latter characterizes the way we can form ourselves through an alternative discourse and disciplined practice.[26] Following Foucault, Talal Asad distinguishes external power (what we do to others) and internal power (what we do to ourselves). Asad attends to what we can do in making/remaking ourselves and others over time.[27] While discourse is central here, so are processes that are both physical and somatic, engaging us in hearing/feeling/seeing/remembering. Calling these procedures an "authorizing discourse," Asad maintains that this process is more than practices of communication alone. They require ritual, meaning by this "the embodiment of conviction," that is, a communal enterprise in which relationships are structured in liturgical-like practices of thinking and acting so that they utilize "a multiplicity of material components."[28] This is what I mean when I speak of formation, of talking the talk and of walking the walk. It is through these kinds of practices that we as subjects take on agency and build internal power. It speaks to the kind of formation for justice that we need in our time.

SUMMARY AND NEXT STEPS

Up to now, I have attempted to elaborate a Christian justice of liberation, mercy, and reconciliation, and to suggest the importance of formation in the development of the sensibilities and dispositions so necessary to this

25. Foucault, *Power/Knowledge*, 106–108.
26. See Foucault, "Technologies of the Self" in *Technologies of the Self,* 16–49.
27. Asad, *Powers of the Secular Modern*, 271.
28. Ibid., 214–16.

justice. Further, I have addressed how important talking the talk and walking the walk are in the discourse and embodiment of a Christian justice. In this chapter I have confronted the key issues of interest and power, unavoidable in any effort to deal with justice and certainly with a Christian justice.

To understand Christian justice as central in the church's life, to operate as people of the new creation, is not to forget that we live in a world with others. It does not mean we disparage others. It does raise the question of how we relate to those of other faith traditions as we respond to the righteousness of God. How do we talk the talk and walk the walk with those who come from other traditions? Do we have anything more than the popular instruction just to be "open"?

Such work with others engages us necessarily with a justice of the common good. This is a justice that works not from the top down but the bottom up, a justice where the marginal, the oppressed, the poor, the excluded, are of first importance. What is a justice of the common good? How do we discover this justice?

Further, by what means can we work with others? I propose that we work through broad-based organizing. To say this does not rule out the value of other undertakings. It offers, rather, an approach that takes seriously the faith traditions out of which people come; it understands the crucial role of their configuration as people of faith and as citizens; it trains people in talking the talk and walking the walk of a justice of the common good; it challenges the linear, unilateral power operative in the coercion and normalcy of the powers, even as it offers a relational power that intercedes in the granular practices of established power and challenges the facades of "truth" that cover domination with abstract intelligibilities that serve the few at the expense of the many. In these ways broad-based organizing opens the door to a new future for those who wish again to be faithful witnesses to the powers and active citizens in the search for the common good.

We turn to these three challenging issues in the final chapter.

Chapter 6

A JUSTICE OF THE COMMON GOOD

In these pages I come from a distinctively Christian understanding of justice, and I make no apology for that. I believe that God has uniquely revealed Self in Jesus Christ and that this divine act is the most profound disclosure and action of God in history. At the same time, I realize that we live in a world with others and that an explicit Christian justice will not speak to those in other traditions. Furthermore, I am not about to claim that God cannot reveal Self to those outside the faith, those in other traditions. Such a claim is beyond my pay grade! Notice here that my hesitancy is centered in God and not because I make claims for other faith traditions that I am not qualified to make. That is, some people say that all of the great faith traditions are equally true. I don't know how anyone would know that. How can one be so formed and informed in all those traditions as to be able to make that kind of claim? We cannot be on all of those journeys at once. Others say, we are all climbing the same mountain just by different routes. Not only do I not know that, but it seems to me to obscure the very real differences among various faith traditions and suggests somehow that one has so transcended the faith traditions of the world that he or she is able to make universal claims on the basis of some "neutral" standpoint that for the life of me I know of no way to establish. So I will go in a different direction. I want to find resources for relating to people who are other by means of the Christian tradition itself, more specifically from Jesus.

JESUS AND OTHERS

I find rich resources in the Christian scriptures for learning from those who are other, but let me be clear here, I am not making a pretense of how "open" I am. I see this issue as one in which I am under the instruction and the witness of Christ. I think it was Stanley Hauerwas who first called my attention to the fact that in the Gospel of Luke (10:25-37), when Christ wants to teach us what love is and what love of neighbor is like, he turns to a Samaritan, someone not only *other* to his own tradition but someone profoundly hated by his own people. Clearly, this is to learn from others, even those hated, at least, by some in one's own tradition.

Or, the story of the centurion and his servant in Luke (7:1-10) where the centurion sends Jewish elders to ask Jesus to come and heal his slave who is sick and close to death. The elders do go to see Jesus and commend the centurion as one who loved the Jewish people and helped build their synagogue for them. As Jesus goes with the elders to the house of the military officer, however, the centurion has had second thoughts and sends word that it is not necessary for Jesus to come, because the centurion feels he is not worthy of Jesus coming into his house. Rather, the centurion states that the situation is like that of his giving orders as a military officer. If he gives an order, it is carried out. He sends word that all Jesus has to do is to speak the word—give the order—and his servant will be healed. Upon hearing the report of this comment by the centurion, Jesus says, "I tell you, not even in Israel have I found such faith." Note, Jesus is speaking here of a military officer who is part of an invading army that occupies Jesus's native land. While he is "worthy" according to the Jewish elders, it is difficult for someone to be more *other* than that!

Or, finally, the parallel stories of the Canaanite woman (Matt 15:21-28) and the Syrophoenician woman (Mark 7:24-30) report a situation where Jesus is asked by a foreign woman to heal her demon-possessed daughter. Jesus responds that he is called to the people of Israel, and uses the metaphor that it is not fair to take the children's food and give it to the dogs. Surely this is one of the hardest things Jesus is reported to say in the Gospels. But the woman is undeterred, as she responds, "Yes, Lord, yet even the dogs eat the crumbs that fall from their master's table." Jesus answers, "Woman, great is your faith. Let it be done to you as you wish." With that her daughter is healed immediately (Matt 15:28). I don't know how you read this story, but I read it as Jesus being taken on—even corrected?—by this woman, a foreigner and one beyond his own faith tradition. This is a powerful story, one with extraordinary implications for our relationships with those of other traditions. I read this story as requiring Christians to take critique from those who are other, even to change our minds.

So from these stories of a Good Samaritan, a centurion, and two foreign women we learn what love and faith are and that we are to receive direction or criticism from those outside our faith tradition. This is no small testimony.

But there is more that I shall only call to mind here. We learn in Hebrews not to neglect hospitality to strangers because by welcoming them we may entertain angels unawares (13:2). Even more, in Matthew 25:31-46 we learn of the Christ who shows up in the hungry, the thirsty, the stranger, the naked, the sick, and the prisoner. As central as Christ is in God's righteous, revelatory, and history-altering act, this God comes to us yet again and again in human need, the alien, physical malady, vulnerable exposure, and the incarcerated. We have much to learn from and we cannot ignore the Christ who stands at the margins. Beyond these, many theologians have made the point that the kingdom of God—the reign, the rule of God—is wider than the church. God is at work in the world, and to follow God, to be in concert with God, is to join that work beyond the boundaries of the church.

PAUL AND THE GOOD OF ALL

Related quite closely to these teachings are Paul's comments about the good of all. It is striking that from his earliest writings (1 Thes 5:15) to his latest (Rom 12:9-21) Paul encourages the members of the ecclesia to pursue not only the good of the household of faith but the good of all. In fact, Paul seems quite diligent in teaching the responsibility of his churches to demonstrate actively their good will and support of those outside the faith. In the important passage of Romans 12 he exhorts the body to be genuine in their love, to offer hospitality to strangers, even to bless those who persecute them. They are called to associate with the lowly and not repay evil for evil, but to take thought for what is noble in the sight of all. They are to live peaceably with all in so far as this is possible. They are not to avenge themselves but to leave vengeance to the Lord. Rather, they are to feed their enemies and give them drink and to overcome evil with good (Rom 12:9-21). Paul is quite clear that the ecclesia are to "work for the good of all" (Gal 6:10).

Furthermore, Paul seems clearly to value certain moral standards in the wider society. As we see above, the congregations are to take thought for what is noble in the sight of all. New Testament scholar Victor Furnish observes that there is a correspondence between the "good" as understood in the wider society and that of people of faith. Again, in Paul's call for the Roman church to be transformed by the renewing of their minds, he calls them to discern the will of God–what is good and acceptable and perfect.

Paul explicitly instructs his church to be "honorable" (1 Thess 4:12) and "noble" (2 Cor 8:21; Rom 12:17b) in the sight of everyone (cf. 1 Cor

5:1, 10:32; Phil 4:5a; Gal 6:10). Not only this, he endorses "whatever" can be described as "praiseworthy" (Phil 4:8) and even calls rulers authorized by God to be servants of "the [public] good." He suggests that members of the churches test everything" in order to "hold fast to what is good" and "abstain from every form of evil" (1 Thess 5:21-22). Clearly convinced of the evil of this present age, he still does not categorically dismiss the moral wisdom of Gentiles or suggest that the ecclesia cannot learn from them. Paul seems to take seriously, says Furnish, that believers are "to take critical account of whatever society in general deems to be good, just, and honorable, and also of whatever it regards as evil, unjust, and shameful."[1] One could go on, but it is clear that Paul urges his young churches to seek the good of those outside of the faith and that there is clearly moral benefit to be found in the teachings and wisdom of the Gentile world, albeit a cosmos ruled by the powers.

Finally, Furnish states explicitly that Paul does not have a concept of the common good as such, and Paul does not encourage his churches to seek such an aim, but Furnish finds in Paul a basis for such efforts and that Paul does, indeed, call for the pursuit of the good of all. This should be enough to suggest that, as utterly convinced as Paul was that God's act in Christ had ultimately delivered the world from the powers and as much as he saw this time between the times as an evil age, he also found reason to call his churches to include everyone in their love and outreach, to learn from and be directed by certain virtues of that world, and to commit to modes of conduct that the Gentile world would find respectable and moral (1 Thess 3:12, 4:12, 5:15; 1 Cor 10:32-33).[2]

It is on the basis of such stories from Jesus and these exhortations of Paul, among many other things that could be said, that I find not only an opening to reach out to others but a mandate. Further, the Apostle Paul opens the door for serious work in pursuit of the common good on the part of the contemporary church. With this we are ready to examine the idea of the common good and to seek a concrete description of it or at least develop a process for its discovery. We turn next to this challenging enterprise.

THE SEARCH FOR THE COMMON GOOD

Let me begin this discussion of the common good by first turning to what may be the biggest danger in its pursuit, which is the danger of

---

1. Furnish, "Uncommon Love and the Common Good," 83–87.
2. Ibid., 87.

turning it into an abstraction where it gains its concreteness when elites of some kind come up with a program, name it as the common good, and then attempt to impose it by organizing a community of some kind or a group or a set of institutions around it. Such a move is virtually guaranteed to fail in terms of bringing genuine good to a local community, especially if that community is relatively powerless and/or poor. I want to suggest a very different way of approaching this matter.

The first thing to be said is that no one knows what the common good is at the beginning of an effort in its behalf. Its determination is a discovery, a process; it is that down on the ground, hard work of listening, and a persistent commitment to hear people into speech. It is that work of mutual storytelling where we discover our passions and our deepest commitments. It is a procedure that must be concrete; abstract notions of distributive justice require suspicion, even distrust. The common good emerges in the building of relationships, in the cultivation of trust, and in the building of organizations of flesh and blood people. It is a procedure where people begin to identify, name, resist, and challenge the powers. Specific to place, the common good is public; it requires people who are local but not parochial.[3] Further, the common good cannot be reducible to individual and group interest; if these interests are always there, there is always more, or, as I contend, self-interest must be understood in a richly social context.[4]

The common good is profoundly political, but not in the degraded way that word is usually employed. By political I mean the way that we organize our lives together. In this sense no set of social relationships is apolitical; the activities of the family, the workings of the neighborhood, life together in the church, the organization of a business or a craft or a school, and those of the economic order and public affairs: all of these are political. In this sense, politics cannot be avoided. Even those who retreat from the organizing of our life together participate in a politics, one of withdrawal, which is a decisive move even if by default. Choosing not to choose is a choice and carries severe political consequences.

---

3. This distinction of local but not parochial is from Charles M. Payne, *I've Got the Light of Freedom*, 101. This extraordinary book is one of the very best one can read about down on the ground organizing in the most difficult circumstances.

4. Stanley Hauerwas first alerted me to the necessity of understanding the common good as a discovery or a find. I am indebted to his discussion of the common good in his *Vision and Virtue*, 235–40. See also his more recent statement in "A Worldly Church," *War and the American Difference*, 140–50.

GRASSROOTS, BOTTOM-UP CHANGE FOR THE COMMON GOOD

Let me suggest, too, that substantive change in this society in behalf of the common good occurs from the bottom up, not typically from the top down. The change we need for the common good will come from the ground up by organizing flesh and blood people.

I contend that this is the most seriously significant way to discover and establish the common good. I recently reread Martin Luther King Jr.'s book, *Stride toward Freedom*. I was amazed once again by the extraordinary down-on-the-ground organizing that took place in Montgomery, Alabama, during the year-long bus boycott back in 1955–56. Some people may think that the civil rights movement was basically large gatherings of people meeting to hear Dr. King speak. While I wish in no way to detract from Dr. King's amazing leadership and oratorical power, one must not miss the organizing work that went on in Montgomery in getting thousands of African American people to their jobs and of developing the organization, the Montgomery Improvement Association, with the capacity to engage and finally win out over a powerful, segregationist economic, political, and cultural order. This organizing effort and many, many more speak to the bottom-up organizing that resulted finally in the Civil Rights Act of 1964 and the Voting Rights Act of 1965.

Or, the women's movement in the country is a good case in point. To go back only as far as the suffragette movement and then into more recent activity is a study of local groups of women and their allies engaged not only in larger movements of women at the national level but the kind of seemingly spontaneous organizing that went on in schools, colleges, churches, and local communities all across this country. The grassroots activity of this effort is powerful testimony to this kind of local and grassroots work so crucial in substantive change.

I must mention, too, the LGBTQ movement in the United States. I have never seen this country change on any issue as fast as it has on this one. Basic to this change is the way in which this movement has peopled the minds of Americans with those who are LGBTQ that they know and love. Yet, again, it is a mistake to miss the kind of organizing that has gone on. I think of hundreds (perhaps thousands) of groups all across the land, of a host of LGBTQ groups, PFLAG, and others, the place of Stonewall as a triggering event, the response to the AIDS crisis, the welcoming work in thousands of churches, the organizing of students and faculty in schools and colleges, and the rising up of community groups—all were central to the changes on this issue.

All of these, and I can mention more, support the importance of bottom-up, grassroots organizing in pursuit of the common good. The importance of these must not be missed. Here, however, I will focus on broad-based organizing as the way to approach the common good in local communities.

BROAD-BASED ORGANIZING

The most famous community organizer in the United States would have to be Saul Alinsky, who began his work in the "Back of the Yards" movement in the thirties. In those early years and up until the eighties, organizing was basically turf based. Alinsky, for example, believed that poverty was an estate and that organizing should occur in a geographical area of poverty.[5] Later, organizing work discovered not only that such organizations were not adequate to face the size, range, and power of the state and big corporate America but that the work needed to include the middle classes, even sometimes the rich. So the work began to stress organizing institutions that included congregations, civic associations, labor unions, and some businesses. With that, broad-based organizing became an organization of organizations that covered a much larger area and a wider range of groups.

For example, in Phoenix the Valley Interfaith Project, an Industrial Areas Foundation project, is made up of thirty-eight institutions and characterizes itself as "diverse religious, cultural, ethnic, and economic elements from the Valley's parishes, congregations, synagogues, and social, civic and employee groups, all of which share a common democratic and Judeo-Christian ethic and concern for quality of life." In Kansas City the Metro Organization for Racial and Economic Equity, a Gamaliel project, is constituted of twenty churches and an immigration rights organization. Like broad-based organizing more generally, these efforts include a variety of organizations with the largest number of organizations being congregations.

Key to broad-based organizing is the training and development of the collective leadership of the organization. This occurs through sessions in which the focus is on the study of key books and articles and on training through a variety of formats that include input, conversation, simulation exercises, and time with experts in a given field.

---

5. Alinsky's classic works on organizing are *Reveille for Radicals* and *Rules for Radicals*.

The basic criterion for a leader is the capacity of a person to deliver people, that is, how many people can a person get to show up at an event or an action. I find this to be a telling criterion for determining leaders. It has a winnowing characteristic that separates the wheat from the chaff. Being able to contribute to turn out and a willingness to do scut work are key in this regard.

Mentoring is a crucial dimension of this training. The organizers in broad-based organizing are themselves professionally trained, mentored, and supervised, and they in turn provide this support for those in the organization. These organizers are constantly on the lookout for people with talent and commitment for citizenship and public life. Not only do they mentor broad-based organizations but they agitate and strategize with them as well. Long time IAF organizer and leader Ed Chambers says, "Their vocation is both simple and profound: to challenge and support citizens and people of belief—democratic or religious—to claim their public selves, to develop their political clout, and to learn how to stand for the whole."[6]

At the very foundation of broad-based organizing are listening and relational meetings, which are why broad-based organizing can have such an important role in both the discovery of the common good and in working for it. Unlike those approaches to change that have an issue already selected and then mainly recruit people for that work, broad-based organizing begins with practices that seek to discern what are the crucial concerns, interests, and values of people. The wisdom of this approach is that elites do not come in with some agenda that they then attempt to impose on people. The imposition of issues on people does not touch the passions, the interests, the motivations, and the central concerns of a people's lives. The kind of organizing envisioned here begins with where people are and builds its strength from the ground up. Basic to this work is the cycle of organizing.

THE CYCLE OF ORGANIZING

Think of the cycle of organizing as a cycle that is ongoing. There are six ingredients in the cycle: one-to-one relational conversations, house meetings, research actions and power analysis, civic academies, public actions,

6. Chambers, *Roots for Radicals*, 66.

and evaluation. We shall consider each of these with a very brief description on their characteristics.[7]

Relational Meetings: *The One-on-One*

It is difficult to exaggerate the importance of listening in the work of broad-based organizing. Listening is the way to find the energy of people, to discover where the issues, the pain, the suffering, the passion, the commitment are. It opens the door to relationships and bonding. Not only these things, but it builds one's compassion and restores motivation for organizing when times are hard and the going is slow.

The most basic practice of organizing is called the *one-on-one* or *one-to-one meeting*. These are sessions in which you meet for thirty to forty minutes with another person. It is a time of sharing stories, especially those stories that indicate where a person is coming from. That is, who is this person? What is the basic story that operates in this person's life? What does she want? Where is this person's passion? What does he give energy to? What special insights does she have? What is this person's self-interest? Does this person have leadership ability? Does this person have a vision?

It is also a time to offer your own stories and yourself so that you begin to build a relationship. Be vulnerable. But remember that you want the other person to talk 60 to 70 percent of the time.

In one-on-ones keep a distinction between probing and prying. Prying is voyeuristic; it is inappropriate curiosity, where curiosity itself becomes an end in itself. A probe attends to the underpinnings of a person's public life: why they are engaged in public action or why not? What story or stories reveal the basic cast of their public relationships or lack thereof? Or, as I would want to know, what are their loves?

A one-on-one is not counseling or therapy. It is not a delving into the personal dynamics of another person with the aim of altering their psychological makeup. It is listening for the captivity of the powers, the places of enslavement, the hurt and pain of oppression, or the grip of normalcy on a person's life. It is the building of a relationship so as to discover whether this person will participate in an organizing effort and, if so, on what basis?

---

7. For more on broad-based organizing see Chambers, *Roots for Radicals*; Michael Gecan, *Going Public*; Stanley Hauerwas and Romand Coles, *Christianity, Democracy and the Radical Ordinary*; Robert Linthicum, *Transforming Power*; William M. Payne, *I've Got the Light of Freedom*; and Jeffrey Stout, *Blessed Are the Organizers*.

It is not the formation of a personal or private friendship. In organizing it is the building of a public friendship, the kind of relationship that can enable both of you to work together in addressing issues critical to the two of you and to others.

One-on-ones are a skill and an art form. They require training and intentional repetition. We are never done in the development of this practice.

The One-on-One and Deep Organizing in a Congregation

In walking the walk, deep organizing in the congregation is another key range of practices. Too many times those interested in justice in a local congregation become the small caucus of people who too often "just talk" or engage in a few social issues that involve hardly anyone else in the congregation. Such groups seldom approach others in the church to discover what their issues are, the places where they are in difficulty, or the concerns they have. What is needed is a time for deep organizing and for an active use of the one-on-one.

There are several ways to proceed here. First, of course, is simply to engage in one-on-ones with people in the congregation. I know of no better way to build relationships with people in a local church. Often, people in a congregation will say they know each other very well. This may or may not be the case. One practice that works effectively is to use one-on-ones in the various gatherings of the church to build relationships between congregants.

Take, for example, the first fifteen to twenty minutes of a board or committee meeting for people to split up into twos and do an abbreviated one-on-one. Instructions for these brief conversations can vary. One suggestion is that they tell the story of their relationship to God. Most people, at least in mainline churches, tend to speak instead of their relationship to the church. Stress the importance of talking about their relationship to God. Also, suggest that they speak with the person in the room that they know least well. Further, direct the group to use story as much as possible in their comments. I recommend that such meetings continue and become a part of most every board and committee meeting. As these meetings continue, the topics can branch out into discussions of issues that affect them, their families, their friends and associates.

A second example is to use one-on-ones in worship venues, especially those with smaller crowds. For example, a Maundy Thursday service can be a good place to make use of one-on-ones. These services often include the washing of feet and the Eucharist. A one-on-one is an appropriate and sensitive way to move into the foot washing time before ending the evening with Holy Communion. Those in each one-on-one would then wash the other's feet. One-on-ones can also be very useful in Bible study groups and other forms of Christian education.

Finally, a suggestion for pastors in local congregations. When a pastor moves initially into a new congregation, I propose that at least one late afternoon and early evening be devoted to one-on-ones with members of the congregation, say, from three to seven o'clock. Members of the congregation can sign up for these on a schedule placed on the bulletin board or kept by a church secretary. If there is great demand, more than one afternoon to evening can be scheduled. This is a very efficient way to get to know people in the congregation and begin building relationships with church members immediately.

The point here, of course, is that one-on-ones enable a deep organizing in the local congregation. After a time, members and pastor become acquainted with each other's story and develop empathy and interest in each other. Further, in terms of justice ministry a determination can be more accurately made of who has interest and passion in this direction and thereby know something of their commitment to it.

Let me say, too, in contrast to the community organizing approach, that in the church we are developing not only a public friendship but a friendship in Christ. This involves us in a more deeply spiritual relationship and offers ties and commitments that surpass those of a public kind. In these relations the commitment to a Christian justice takes on conviction and a compelling call to engagement in the practices of liberation, mercy, and reconciliation. Again, these may not be typically personal friendships—though some are—but congregational friendships in Christ.

House Meetings

Yet another practice in community organizing is that of the house meeting. These are usually meetings of eight to twelve people designed to determine the issues with which people struggle. In some cases church members are invited to a church supper. After the meal the crowd is divided up into small groups of an appropriate size. If the crowd is around one hundred people, groups of about eight are good. If it is a smaller crowd, the groups can be about six people. In each group there should be one coordinator to keep people on topic and another person to take notes. The coordinator makes it clear that the purpose of the group is to hear each person's experience with a given issue. The session must not become one of advice giving or helping to solve the problem. The purpose instead is to hear each person's situation, especially encouraging them to describe their experience in terms of stories. This is also not a time for argument or for critique. It is a time to listen. Notice, by the way, that it is hard to critique a story.

During the housing crisis of 2008 in Arizona one church used the sermon time during the worship service for small group meetings. The pastor read a biblical text, made a brief comment about that text in relationship to housing, and then organized the congregation into small groups of six. The gathering was then asked to discuss in their small group meeting the impact of the housing crisis on them personally, their family, their friends, or people at work. The session went for about twenty-five minutes, the usual length of the pastor's sermon. Later we were shocked that *every* person in the room had a story from their lives about the impact of the housing crisis on them or someone they knew. This is a powerfully useful way for a congregation to get in touch with each other and also to know what people are dealing with. It also can build energy and motivation to get involved in organizing around serious matters facing a congregation. Like one-on-ones, it is also a good place to discover those with leadership capacities and with passion for a given issue.

Power Analysis and Research Actions

Relational meetings and house meetings are good ways to find out where people are and to discover issues that affect their lives. The concept of an issue here is important. Broad-based organizing makes a distinction between an issue and a problem. An issue is something you can do something about; a problem is something that is too big, too encompassing to address. For example, an issue would be the use of a toxic dump in a neighborhood that is creating sickness and even death; a problem would be the ecological crisis. Through the organizing of a community, there is plenty that can be done about a toxic dump, but the ecological crisis cannot be addressed unless you break it down into winnable issues.

The determination of a winnable issue requires an internal power analysis of the capacity of your own organizing group. Does the group have the required number of leaders and followers with self-interest around the issue who can effectively take it on? Will they mobilize and turn out in the critical mass required to have the necessary impact on the opposing forces? Is this the right time? Who will line up with your organization? What conversations are needed with potential allies? Will this effort and the organizing necessary help to build the power of the organization, which is crucial to civic life and public action? Can it be done?

An external power analysis is also necessary. Who are those in positions of power that are key decision makers who may be opponents? What allies will they have? What will their likely response be? Will opposition be a major response from them? Will they simply blow you off?

These power analyses are accompanied by research actions, which usually consist of conversations with authorities in a given field, with public officials who work in the relevant arenas, and with those who have extensive relationships with people dealing with the issue. These research actions are a time for a group to do careful research and to be deeply informed about the issue.

How do you know when you have completed a research action? There is a good rule of thumb. When you begin these conversations, you will hear names and suggestions of people to go and see. After a good many conversations, you will begin to hear the names of those you have already met with. When you are not hearing new names, you have probably talked with the relevant people. Then you are ready for a civic academy.

Civic Academies

Civic academies are opportunities to bring together clergy, leaders, key experts, and resource people in a given field for intentional, structured dialogue around issues that emerge from one-on-ones, house meetings, and research actions. The object here is to break through the kind of public relations and promotional pitches that so often characterize the media and public posturing and to provide significant dialogue, deeper engagement with the issues, and the building of a wider range of relationships.

Experts and resource people can include government officials, professors with significant research knowledge, key nonprofit figures, union leaders, business people, and so on.

Presentations are made for the purpose of informing the participants on the issue at hand. In response to these presentations, participants then break out in small groups so that they can process the input with more in-depth conversation, the sharing of stories, the raising of new questions, suggestions for follow up actions, and commitment to action. The group then regathers as a whole, concluding with brief summaries of the findings of each group, the proposals for next steps, and the communication of commitments made by members of the group.

These academies are highly structured in order to make sure that the time is well spent. Long speeches by resource people are ruled out; the idea is to get to the nub of what is important in a presentation. Small groups are carefully led to avoid the domination of discussions by one or two people. The meeting begins on time and ends on time, usually about an hour and a half.

Actions

Relational and house meetings, research actions, and civic academies lead to actions. An action can be a meeting of several hundred or several thousand people. It is a public drama, where a winnable issue is presented, typically with stories from people who struggle with the issue in their families and everyday life. For example, stories are told by people who work long and hard and can't make a living for their families because of a low minimum wage, or people who get good job training and then can't find a job.

The agenda of the broad-based organization is a direct response to the struggles of these flesh-and-blood people. The meeting then raises these issues with key government officials, business executives, and other public representatives who are asked straightforwardly if they will support the agenda of the broad-based organization. Informed ahead of time, the public figure knows exactly which questions she or he will be asked and of the time he or she will have to respond. The questions basically ask if this person will support the agenda of the broad-based organization. The questions ask for a public commitment.

The large gathered group is trained in a premeeting to respond actively to the public officials and to do so vigorously so that they cheer loudly for figures who affirm the agenda, and heartily oppose a negative or unsupportive answer.

Obviously, these events are well planned and scripted in order to make them succinct and to accurately frame the issue and the questions asked. The stories too are scripted for economy of expression. The session moves. Again, long speeches are forbidden. Over communication is miscommunication. In length the actions go for an hour to an hour and a half.

Evaluation

I address evaluation last in the cycle of organizing, but it is a pervasive practice throughout every phase of the cycle. It is typically the last thing done in every meeting of any kind except for the prayer. Evaluations are done after a meeting but not with those outside the organization. For example, an evaluation of an action is not done in the presence of the public officials who were questioned.

One format that seems especially helpful is to ask everyone in the evaluative session to say one word that characterizes her or his feeling as a response to the meeting. Individuals may say things like, *encouraged, disappointed, hopeful, confused, troubled, excited,* and so forth. The evaluator can then follow up specific words by asking the person to elaborate. This relatively brief session can then be followed by asking for comments on how the chair, the organizer, or presenters in the meeting performed, or how the entire group did.

The more that evaluation becomes simply what an organization does the better. The greater the candor the better. The more that the critique is meant to help and the greater the trust the better. Critique is a gift, so be generous. This certainly applies to organizing. Evaluation is especially important in the mentoring and apprenticeship functions of organizing, but it is crucial throughout the work.

SUMMARY

In summary, a Christian justice of liberation, mercy, and reconciliation takes us into a world where there are people who do not share our convictions. They come out of different faith traditions and some out of a secular and/or atheist commitment. I have argued that in Jesus we find ourselves instructed and even critiqued, or at least challenged, by those who are other, and in Paul we discover grounds for seeking the good of all, not an espousal of the common good as such, but surely an opening door to that aim. Further, I insist with others that the common good is a discovery, a find, something that does not come through elite strategies from the top down but rather through a grassroots, bottom-up approach that privileges listening to flesh and blood people to determine the suffering, the pain, the issues, and the needs they have in their communities. I then advocate an approach to the common good in these terms through broad-based organizing where the cycle of organizing is the primary tool.

With these things said, I will now bring these rumination to an end. To do so we turn to a conclusion to draw together some of the connections between a Christian justice and the common good.

CONCLUSION

In these final pages I wish to draw connections between a Christian justice and a justice of the common good. I say draw connections because systematizing these relationships is a bad idea. The totalizing propensities of systemizing such connections closes off not only creative innovations that go beyond the system but can cause us to miss the movement of God in new directions. So instead I will illustrate places where a Christian justice and one of the common good come together. To do so I will make the connections of the common good to each of the dimensions of a Christian justice: deliverance/liberation, mercy, and reconciliation.

First, I find a powerful connection between a Christian justice and the common good around resistance to the principalities and powers that so dominate our lives. When we struggle in common with those of other traditions against these dominations, I find new orbs of deliverance, new ways to understand and enact emancipative actions, some of them so very simple in implementation yet so clearly right. I remember that a man, a Sikh, in Phoenix was shot and killed because his murderer thought he was a Muslim. To support and protect his family, members of the Arizona Interfaith Movement simply took lawn chairs and sat in the driveway of the man's home all through the night. The people there were of different faith traditions and one person was an atheist. While the religious commitments and the reasons people were there were different, they nevertheless came to challenge such violent expressions and to embody an alternative by taking up overnight residence in a driveway.

Certainly not unrelated to such resistance is the naming of the principalities and powers—"the demons"—that operate in our world and in ourselves. In this important work we can be instructed and critiqued by others so that we come to a sharper-edged nomenclature, a vocabulary that opens up points of resistance and action. Such naming, such fluency is crucial in countering the powers. But these are also occasions where people are given voice and find avenues for action. I have seen people—marginalized all their lives—literally trembling when they have confronted a legislator or the CEO of a corporation, but with the support and training of broad-based organizing they become verbally equipped, poised, and capacious leaders and spokespeople, able to hold their own and address the powers that dominate their lives.

Further, I think of Loomer's concept of relational power as both a tool and a resource for a Christian approach to living out deliverance and liberation. The rich sources of compassion and devotion that flow from life in Christ can readily participate in the mutualities and reciprocities of a shared work with others for the common good. And Foucault's descriptions of what I call the granular practices of power open up a conceptual field for the generation of multiple approaches to the common good that alter the established order of the dominant principalities. Meanwhile, changes in the micro discourses and visible practices of a community reconstitute the strategic relations and the flows of power in a community. As we saw in chapter 4, when the chief of police of Phoenix began neighborhood walks with VIP, the broad-based organization there, the practices and relational power were changed. The long-term work of broad-based organizing can reshuffle, can reconstitute the complex relations of myriads of practices of discourse, of policies and procedures, and regimens.

Second, the practices of mercy are tissues in the relation of a Christian justice and the common good. The discourse and acts of mercy populate the work of broad-based organizing not only in hospitable listening but in receiving the stories embodied in the very lives of the people whom we come to know. In public friendships we find mercies given and received. I remember a meeting where a woman dissolved into tears as she blamed herself that her son had gone to prison. Having struggled all of her life with devastating poverty, she had worked at two minimum-wage jobs to feed, house, and provide for her three children, which, in spite of her best efforts, took her away from home and left her children too much to the wiles of the street. Yet, even under such overwhelming circumstance, she was captive to a self-blame. But that same woman became involved in an organizing effort for the minimum wage. She became trained and then skilled in the cycles of organizing. This work that not only brought release from the false guilt that had incarcerated her gave her names and social policies, and the identification of institutions of principalities and powers that held her captive. These capacities opened ways for her with the support of others to take them on, so that her life did not devolve into false guilt and self-condemnation. It is easy to miss the mercies that operate in the cycles of organizing. We receive mercy as people share their lives with us and join together in the work of the common good.

Mercy also operates in the organizing proverb that there are no permanent enemies or permanent allies, ever reminding us of the impermanence of anything in this life save the coming righteousness of God and a rule of justice and love. A Christian justice reminds us also that no enmity will stand finally before God's power to tear down the walls of hostility that divide us between the times. Equally important, we remember as well that the powers operate in both the church and in broad-based organizing, so that we ever require mercy no matter how right we sometimes think we are or how much we need God's mercy to break the captivities that enslave us in the times and places of our lives.

I need to say something as well about mercy and failure. God's action in Christ resulted initially in crucifixion. It was three days later before resurrection came. Further, we still await Christ's coming again and the completion of the creation. It should come as no surprise that the pursuit of a Christian justice and its work for the common good is a way of life characterized by significant occasions of failure. Organized relationships can fall apart. You can work desperately hard on a given issue and lose. You may need a major turnout of people in order to make a strategic impact on government officials and then be unable to get it. And, sometimes, it is because you did not work hard enough or thoughtfully enough, or skillfully enough. You simply failed. I remember those times graphically. I am helped by another proverb in this work that says all organizing is reorganizing, suggesting that things do fall apart and renewed building of relationships and working again through the cycle of organizing are required. I have found this proverb to be a major pronouncement of mercy.

Finally, broad-based organizing can be a form of reconciliation expressed in a justice of the common good. It reaches across lines of race and class, across the walls of exclusion that prevent a consideration of the wider common good, and across conflicted and diverse interests—really the loves—that characterize our communities. By challenging the powers and by building power from the ground up, new relations open to our communities and strange bedfellows suddenly work together to establish common good. The church is called to a ministry of reconciliation, and broad-based organizing is one form that ministry takes.

The complexities of the organizing cycle open doors to reconciliation—not only the listening that occurs in relational meetings and the stories that open public friendships but the building of trust and working commitments that develop with experts in the field. These can become ongoing commitments to cooperative efforts not to be dismissed in the important work of building the common good by crossing barriers that previously divided us from others. I think of building a relationship with a high state official in Arizona. We worked for two years with him, engaging him in civic academies we held, seeking him out for good information on banks and other financial institutions, and listening to his own frustrations and desire to do more. He was a conservative, Republican, Mormon. I am none of those descriptors, but I shall never forget the day when he had worked carefully with us and had helped us to get a significant decision made. As we left his office, he said, "You know, Tex, I feel one with you because of our relationship to Christ. We have more working for us in all these things. It means a lot to me." Well, that's more than only a public friendship, but what is important to see here is that it came through a research action that we had devoted two years to develop. It is because of events like these that I have come to believe that the cycle of organizing can very much be a means of grace.

At the same time, I recognize that broad-based organizing requires conflict and the naming of opponents, even enemies, just as I recall that Jesus always had enemies. In a Christian justice there is ever the challenge of the powers and tension between the liberation that has come in Christ and the reconciliation to which we are called, so that we are ever pulled by both deliverance from one dimension of God's righteousness and reconciliation from another. And both deliverance and reconciliation are family members of mercy.

Can there be a conflict, a contradiction, between a Christian justice and a justice of the common good? Perhaps, but I cannot find a single place in the writings of the Apostle Paul where he suggests that the good of all flies in the face of the good of the household of faith. My own experience in working in community is that when we find such a conflict, we have more work to do either on our understanding of Christian justice or on the discovery of the common good. We do not have to forsake a Christian justice to pursue the common good with others. That God's justice has been put right in Christ is clear, that we are called to seek the good of all is inescapable. To work out such things is as important as anything I know.

Let me be clear, these few points and illustrations do not exhaust the possible connections between a Christian justice and the common good, but rather are suggestive of directions and possibilities. Indeed, the resources of broad-based organizing bring practices of formation, talking the talk, and walking the walk desperately needed in our time to resist and challenge the powers. In these practices we join others to discover the common good but also to learn what love is, what faith is, and to be challenged and called into account. It is a summons to work with those on the margins, convinced that we find Christ in these locations. In these places we seek to find what God is doing outside the church. We live out the divine comedy where we insinuate ourselves into the plot lines of the powers, and perform a different story. The point here is not that broad-based organizing will bring in a final expression of a Christian justice or the common good. We continue to live between the times in the struggle between the world as it is and the world as it ought to be, but there are shades of difference in the darkness of the night. There are starry nights to counter those devoid of light, and there are mornings brighter than the day before. There are important gains to be made in the relativities of history and the dominations of our time. But God will ultimately complete this creation as the plane of history is taken fully into the divine life. The powers will be defeated. Meanwhile, the church is called by the Spirit to be the new creation, to live out a justice of liberation, mercy, and reconciliation. There are formations of ourselves to be configured, talk to be talked, walks to be walked, and discoveries of the common good to be made and established with others. This is sufficient illumination to go on.

BIBLIOGRAPHY

Augustine of Hippo. *The City of God against the Pagans*. Bk. XIV, Chap. xxviii.

Alinsky, Saul D. *Reveille for Radicals*. Chicago: University of Chicago Press, 1946.

———. *Rules for Radicals: A Pragmatic Primer for Realistic Radicals*. New York: Random House, 1971.

Asad, Talal. *Formations of the Secular: Christianity, Islam, Modernity*. Palo Alto: Stanford University Press, 2003.

———. *Genealogies of Religion: Discipline and Reasons of Power in Christianity and Islam*. Baltimore: Johns Hopkins University Press, 1993.

Bailey, Kenneth E. *Poet & Peasant and Through Peasant Eyes: A Literary-Cultural Approach to the Parables in Luke*. Grand Rapids, MI: Wm. B. Eerdmans, 1983.

Belafonte, Harry. *My Song: A Memoir*. New York: Alfred A. Knopf, 2011.

Bell, Daniel M., Jr. "Jesus, the Jews, and the Politics of God's Justice." *Ex Auditu* 22 (2006): 87–112.

Berry, Wendell. "Caught in the Middle." *Christian Century* (March 20, 2013), 30–31.

Carder, Kenneth L. *Living Our Beliefs: The United Methodist Way*. Nashville: Discipleship Resources, 2014.

Caro, Robert A. *The Years of Lyndon Johnson: Master of the Senate*. New York: Vintage Books, 2003.

Cavanaugh, William. *Migrations of the Holy: God, State, and the Political Meaning of the Church*. Grand Rapids, MI: Wm. B. Eerdmans, 2011.

Chambers, Edward T. *Roots for Radicals: Organizing for Power, Action, and Justice*. London: The Continuum International, 2004.

Cortes, Ernesto. "Reweaving the Social Fabric." *Boston Review*. June/September 1994. http://new.bostonreview.net/BR19.3/cortes.html.

Edwards, James C. *The Authority of Language: Heidegger, Wittgenstein, and the Threat of Philosophical Nihilism.* Tampa: University of Southern Florida, 1990.

Felder, Cain Hope. "The Letter to Philemon: Introduction, Commentary, and Reflections." In *The New Interpreter's Bible.* Edited by Leander E. Keck, 11:833–905. Nashville: Abingdon Press, 2003.

Fletcher, Joseph. *Situation Ethics: The New Morality.* Louisville: Westminster John Knox, 1966.

Flowers, John, and Karen Vannoy. *Not a One Night Stand.* Nashville: Abingdon Press, 2009.

Flynn, Bernard. "Maurice Merleau-Ponty." *The Stanford Encyclopedia of Philosophy.* Fall 2011. Edited by Edward N. Zalta. http://plato.stanford.edu/archives/fall2011/entries/merleau-ponty/.

Foucalt, Michel. *Power/Knowledge: Selected Interviews and Other Writings, 1972–1977.* New York: Pantheon, 1980.

Furnish, Victor Paul. *The Moral Teaching of Paul: Selected Issues.* 2nd ed. Nashville: Abingdon Press, 1985.

———. *Theology and Ethics in Paul.* Nashville: Abingdon Press, 1968.

———. "Uncommon Love and the Common Good: Christians as Citizens in the Letters of Paul." In *In Search of the Common Good.* Edited by Dennis P. McCann and Patrick D. Miller. New York: T & T Clark, 2005.

Gaillard, Frye. "The Gospel according to Will." *Perspectives in Religious Studies* 39, no. 2 (June 1, 2012): 161–72.

Galbraith, John Kenneth. *The Affluent Society.* New York: Houghton Mifflin Harcourt, 1958.

Gaventa, Beverly Roberts. *Our Mother Saint Paul.* Louisville: Westminster John Knox, 2007.

Gecan, Michael. *Going Public: An Organizer's Guide to Citizen Action.* Norwell, MA: Anchor Press, 2004.

Goethe, J. W. Von. *Theory of Color in Scientific Studies.* In vol. 12 of Goethe: *Collected Works in English.* Edited and translated by Douglas Miller. New York: Suhrkamp, 1988.

Greenway, William, and Lee A. Wetherbee. "Vocabularies Matter." *Theological Education* 44, no. 2 (2009): 1–9.

Griffiths, Paul. "Witness and Conviction in *With the Grain of the Universe.*" *Modern Theology* 19 (2003): 67–75.

Hauerwas, Stanley. "Discipleship as a Craft, Church as a Disciplined Community," *Christian Century* (October 1, 1991): 881–84.

———. *Vision and Virtue: Essays in Christian Ethical Reflection.* Notre Dame: Fides Publishers, 1974.

———. *War and the American Difference: Theological Reflections on Violence and National Identity.* Ada, MI: Baker Academic Press, 2011.

———. *Working with Words: On Learning to Speak Christian.* Eugene, OR: Cascade Books, 2011.

Hauerwas, Stanley, and Romand Coles. *Christianity, Democracy, and the Radical Ordinary: Conversations between a Radical Democrat and a Christian.* Eugene, OR: Cascade Books, 2012.

Hays, Richard. *First Corinthians.* Interpretation: A Bible Commentary for Teaching and Preaching. Louisville: John Knox, 1997.

———. "The Liberation of Israel in Luke-Acts." In *Reading the Bible Intertextually.* Edited by Richard B. Hays, Stefan Alkier, and Leroy A. Huizenga, 101-18. Waco, TX: Baylor University Press, 2009.

Hirschman, Albert O. *The Passions and the Interests: Political Arguments for Capitalism before Its Triumph.* Princeton: Princeton University Press, 1977.

———. *Rival Views of Market Society and Other Recent Essays.* Cambridge: Harvard University Press, 1992.

Johnston, David Cay. *Free Lunch: How the Wealthiest Americans Enrich Themselves at Government Expense (and Stick You with the Bill).* New York: Portfolio, 2007.

Jones, L. Gregory. "Maison Shalom," *Christian Century* (June 16, 2009): 29.

Kahneman, Daniel. *Thinking, Fast and Slow.* New York: Farrar, Straus and Giroux, 2011.

Katongole, Emmanuel. *The Sacrifice of Africa: A Political Theology for Africa.* Grand Rapids, MI: Eerdmans Ekklesia Series, 2010.

Lewis, John. *Walking with the Wind: A Memoir of the Movement.* New York: Simon Shuster Paperbacks, 1998.

Linthicum, Robert. *Transforming Power: Biblical Strategies for Making a Difference in Your Community.* Downers Grove, IL: IVP Books, 2003.

Loomer, Bernard. "Two Conceptions of Power," *Process Studies* 6, no. 6 (Spring 1976): 5–32.

MacIntyre, Alasdair. *After Virtue: A Study in Moral Theory.* 2nd ed. Notre Dame: University of Notre Dame Press, 1984.

Marquardt, Manfred. *John Wesley's Social Ethics: Praxis and Principles*. Nashville: Abingdon Press, 1992.

Martin, Christel. *La haine n'aura pas le derniere mot: Maggy la femme aux 10,000 enfants*. Paris: Albin Michel, 2005; unpublished translation by Trent Dailey-Chwalibog and David Dimas.

Martin, Dale B. *Slavery as Salvation: The Metaphor of Slavery in Pauline Christianity*. New Haven: Yale University Press, 1990.

Martin, Luther, Huck Gutman, and Patrick Hutton, eds. *Technologies of the Self: A Seminar with Michel Foucault*. Amhurst: University of Massachusetts Press, 1988.

Martyn, J. Louis. *Galatians: A New Translation with Introduction and Commentary*. Anchor Bible 33A. New York: Doubleday, 1997.

Milbank, John. *Theology and Social Theory: Beyond Secular Thinking*. Oxford, UK: Basil Blackwell Ltd., 1990.

Miles, Sara. *Take This Bread: A Radical Conversion*. New York: Random House 2007.

The Miracle Worker. Directed by Arthur Penn, screenplay by William Gibson, starring Anne Bancroft and Patty Duke, 1962.

Ong, Walter J. *The Presence of the Word*. Minneapolis: University of Minnesota Press, 1967.

Payne, Charles M. *I've Got the Light of Freedom*. Oakland: University of California Press, 2007.

Ramsey, Paul. *Basic Christian Ethics*. Louisville: Westminster John Knox, 1993.

Roof, Wade Clark. *Spiritual Marketplace: Baby Boomers and the Remaking of American Religion*. Princeton: Princeton University Press, 1999.

Royce, Edward. *Poverty and Power*. Lanham, MD: Rowman and Littlefield Publishers, Inc. 2009.

Sample, Tex. *Human Nature, Interest, and Power: A Critique of Reinhold Niebuhr's Social Thought*. Eugene OR: Cascade Books, 2013.

Scott, David, and Charles Hirschkind, eds. *Powers of the Secular Modern: Talal Asad and His Interlocutors*. Palo Alto: Stanford University Press, 2006.

Smith, Christian, Kari Christoffersen, Hilary Davidson, Patricia Snell Herzog. *Lost in Transition: The Dark Side of Emerging Adulthood*. New York: Oxford University Press, 2011, 80.

Stark, Rodney. *The Rise of Christianity: How the Obscure, Marginal Jesus*

Movement Became the Dominant Religious Force in the Western World in a Few Centuries. San Francisco: Harper, 1997.

Stiglitz, Joseph. "There Is No Invisible Hand," *The Guardian,* Dec. 20, 2002.

Stout, Jeffrey. *Blessed Are the Organized: Grassroots Democracy in America.* Princeton: Princeton University Press, 2012.

Wesley, John. Sermon 72, "Of Evil Angels." In the *Sermons of John Wesley.* Nampa, ID: Northwest Nazarene University Wesley Center for Applied Theology, 1998. http://wesley.nnu.edu/sermons-essays-books/.

Williams, Daniel Day. *The Spirit and Forms of Love.* Lanham, MD: University Press of America, 1981.

Wills, Gary. *Lincoln at Gettysburg: The Words That Remade America.* New York: Simon Schuster, 1992.

Witherington, Ben, III. *Conflict and Community in Corinth.* Grand Rapids, MI: Wm. B. Eerdmans Publishing Company, 1995.

Yankelovich, Daniel. *New Rules: Searching for Self-Fulfillment in a World Turned Upside Down.* New York: Bantam Books, 1984.

Zajonc, Arthur. *Catching the Light: The Entwined History of Light and Mind.* New York: Bantam, 1993.

Zinn, Howard. *A People's History of the United States.* New York: Harper Perennial Modern Classics, 2005.

INDEX

CPSIA information can be obtained
at www.ICGtesting.com
Printed in the USA
LVOW12s0124220316

480149LV00003B/3/P